PRAISE FOR *KEEP YOUR CUSTOMERS*

"We wanted to understand accurately the cost we were incurring with our ad campaign, the goal of which was to encourage a woman to visit our store and buy her first pair of Stuart Weitzman shoes. It came to $8000, and we sold her a $500 pair, on average. The second pair she bought from us, later in the season or the following one, cost us nothing. Such an investment is obviously only worthwhile if the goal is to establish a long-term relationship with this new customer. That is why a wonderful customer experience and a product that does what we say it will, are the pillars of retail. As Ali Cudby illustrates so well, creating that experience is a business decision and a business opportunity. Whether you sell shoes, toothpaste or technology, you want your customers to keep buying, and *Keep Your Customers* will show you how. A terrific read!"

—STUART WEITZMAN, Shoe Guru

"*Keep Your Customers* fits perfectly into the mission and growth plans of any brand that wants to keep its customers for life. In addition to providing a toolkit around purpose and vision, segmentation, and the importance of data, what I found particularly resonant for brands like Weight Watchers, Girls Scouts or the NFL, where I've had the pleasure of working, are her insights, tips and tools around establishing an emotional connection with customers and team members through celebration. She aptly recognizes this is the key to driving high word of mouth and repeat business and longevity of service. Ali Cudby's process is an actionable guide for any business leader aiming for best practices with their customers. If you want to keep your customers for the long-term, everyone in your company should read this book."

—DANNY BOOCKVAR, Former Pr

"Our influence boils down to what we do and what we celebrate. Ali shows us how to influence thoughtfully and compassionately—all with the aim of creating strong relationships and solid businesses."

—**MAX YODER**, CEO of Lessonly and bestselling author of *Do Better Work*

"Ali Cudby has written a playbook for customer retention that is both entertaining and easy to implement. Whether you are working on your first startup or the CEO of a Fortune 500 company, *Keep Your Customers* provides actionable advice that can create noticeable improvements to your business. Every business leader should read this book."

—**KATLYN GRASSO**, CEO and Founder of GenHERation

"The path to maximizing customer lifetime value tends to focus on either emotional engagement or the power of data and analytics. In *Keep Your Customers*, Ali Cudby demonstrates why you need both to build strong relationships between brands and consumers. Then she shows you exactly how to turn that idea into your company's reality, with case studies and step by step guidelines to make it easy to implement. *Keep Your Customers* is a blueprint that can be used by startups, large corporations and everyone in between."

—**SAPNA SHAH**, angel investor and founder of Retail X Series

"Well researched, practical and eye-opening, *Keep Your Customers* demystifies customer loyalty and shows you how to make it your new reality. By giving equal time to the connection of customer relationship and the data needed on the back-end to make process work seamlessly, Ali Cudby's approach is unique. Whether your company sells to consumers or other businesses, you'll find gold inside these pages. This book is a fantastic resource for any business leader. It isn't leaving my desk!"

—**DAVE DUKE**, Co-Founder & Chief Customer Officer at MetaCX

"Proper customer identification, conversion and retention are crucial for scaling a business and for long-term profitability. In *Keep Your Customers*, Ali Cudby unpacks a useful guide to long-term customer loyalty that's engaging, insightful and actionable. The stories, case studies and her practical approach make it a fast, easy read. Anyone seeking to raise venture capital and to build a sustainable business should read this book."

—**JONATHAN TOWER**, Managing Partner at Catapult VC

"Developing customer loyalty isn't the result of a single moment, it's an outcome of daily execution throughout every part of a company. That's easier to say than do. Ali Cudby lays out the strategic thinking and ongoing processes companies need to establish and sustain long-term customers. This book shows you how to become a trusted advisor in a way that sets you apart from your competition. If you care about long-term customer relationships, *Keep Your Customers* lays out straightforward path to success."

—**JAMES "JA" A. HILLEBRAND**, CEO of Stock Yards Bank & Trust Co. and Stock Yards Bancorp, Inc.

"Ali Cudby expertly captures the important priorities that are so easily overlooked preventing many companies from institutionalizing the right behaviors. This book provides insights into the right areas of focus and provides the why behind them in addition to sharing real relatable examples. It blows the other books on customer loyalty out of the water. Read it immediately and then get copies to everyone in your company so you can all use the *Keep Your Customers* playbook."

—**TIM CONDER**, Senior Director Client Innovation, Zotec Partners

"Ali Cudby's book belongs on the shelf of every business leader charged with improving the customer experience. Complete with practical suggestions and illustrative examples, this work describes how to make a 'Heart and Smart' customer experience that retains and grows customer relationships."

—**ED POWERS**, CX and Customer Success
expert in the technology sector

"*Keep Your Customers* provides a practical map to navigating one of the biggest roadblocks facing companies today – retaining customers for long-term, profitable relationships. Ali Cudby offers a compelling framework and combines it with actionable tactics to break down the obstacles to progress into manageable steps any company can tackle successfully. This book a must-read primer for any leader who wants to improve long-term customer value."

—**HANIEL LYNN**, CEO, Kastle Systems

KEEP YOUR CUSTOMERS

KEEP YOUR CUSTOMERS

How to Stop Customer Turnover, Improve Retention, and Get Lucrative, Long-Term Loyalty

ALI CUDBY

NEW YORK

LONDON • NASHVILLE • MELBOURNE • VANCOUVER

KEEP YOUR CUSTOMERS

How to Stop Customer Turnover, Improve Retention and Get Lucrative, Long-Term Loyalty

Published in New York, New York, by Morgan James Publishing. Morgan James is a trademark of Morgan James, LLC. www.MorganJamesPublishing.com

ISBN 9781642796421 paperback
ISBN 9781642796438 eBook
Library of Congress Control Number: 2019943449

Cover Design by:
Christopher Kirk
www.GFSstudio.com

Interior Design by:
Chris Treccani
www.3dogcreative.net

Morgan James is a proud partner of Habitat for Humanity Peninsula and Greater Williamsburg. Partners in building since 2006.

Get involved today! Visit
MorganJamesPublishing.com/giving-back

DEDICATION

To Dad, whose example taught me the value of loyalty.

"Life is like a path that winds around a mountain, from base to summit. Your journey up the path continually brings you back to the same vista, each time from a slightly different perspective."

–Unknown

TABLE OF CONTENTS

FOREWORD

When I met Ali, she was in college, and I was the CEO of USA Networks. She was exploring a career in entertainment and was inspired by storytelling that had enough emotional heft to motivate people. We reconnected later when she was finishing her MBA at the Wharton School and heading off to work in strategic planning at The New York Times Company. She was shifting to the corporate side of media and still motivated by businesses that made a difference.

In one way or another, Ali has been focused on the balance between connecting with people and applying business rigor for long-term profitability since she was an undergraduate. This book is the natural evolution of everything she has talked about and accomplished since then. It's also a message that is vitally important for business leaders. Today more than ever, connectedness is paramount to success. It's something I have layered into every company I've managed, but having this book would have helped me.

At USA Networks the advertisers were our customers. Our success with them depended on attracting viewers, as it does today. In the '80s, there were only a few television networks, which meant audiences had a limited number of choices if they wanted to watch television. As a network, we could take time to attract viewers to a show. Over the course of a couple of seasons, we would hone storylines and characters to make them more compelling to audiences, whether they loved them or loved to hate them. Looking back, the idea that we had a season—or two—to refine shows until they became fully realized stories for their audiences seems like a luxury. Having time meant we could establish relationships with viewers, and the better we understood our viewers, the better we could craft shows that would bring them back again and again.

But times have changed. Companies have to connect faster than ever before.

When I was non-executive chairman of Liz Claiborne, we owned the Kate Spade brand. Kate Spade stood out because it had a much larger brand presence than the size of the company would indicate. We saw how the company grew affinity by speaking clearly to its customers. It was a niche approach, and the brand's voice was laser-focused on a relatively small group. Because Kate Spade targeted its niche so successfully, customers loved the brand. As a result, Kate Spade was able to build more stores and grow the business more than ten-fold in a short period of time. All because their messaging made an emotional connection with their consumers.

Ali has a strong point of view on customer engagement, the holy grail of keeping and improving your relationship with your customer.

In this book, Ali shares a key truth: customers who feel valued are more likely to become loyal. Loyal customers are vastly preferable to casual ones. To cultivate those all-important connected relations with customers, companies need data, process, and training to deliver consistently strong results. They need to know which customers are most valuable and tailor the experience to the most valuable customer cohort. All customers are not created equal. To do this effectively, companies need to track, measure, and consistently improve. They need both heart and smart.

I see business leaders undercutting the value of emotional connection as a lever for customer loyalty. Some see emotion as the opposite of data—they think "data-driven" is always the best approach. Some shy away from talking about emotion because it is uncomfortable for them. What I've seen throughout my career, and what Ali's book expertly highlights, is that emotional connection is essential for building relationships. Companies that avoid knowing their customers well enough to deliver what they want will struggle to build momentum.

Companies spend billions getting people to know, like, trust, try, and buy what they sell for the first time (customer acquisition). Billions are spent, often with questionable results. Spending money to get customers—and creating so-so programs to keep them— won't build profitable customer relationships for the long term. These days, it's just not enough to generate affinity.

From the worlds of retail, entertainment, technology, and beyond, this book shares both Ali's philosophy and the actionable steps she believes you need to take to create connected relationships with your customers. Ali's case studies show the way. The lessons she lays out resonate with my personal experiences at companies like USA Networks and multi-national retailer Kate Spade.

After you've read Keep Your Customers, you'll have a roadmap to your best customers, a team engaged with your vision, and a clear path to success. In Ali's connected world, everybody wins.

Kay Koplovitz,
Founder of Springboard Enterprises

Author of *Been There, Run That* and *Bold Women, Big Ideas: Learning to Play the High-Risk Entrepreneurial Game*

INTRODUCTION

I n 2004, a bra fitting changed my life. I walked into a lingerie store and had a customer experience that transformed my self-image. It inspired me personally, and I couldn't stop talking about it. I started writing about the importance of good bras and good fit. Much to my surprise, that moment in a Cambridge, United Kingdom, bra store transformed me professionally as well. I decided every woman could have an experience similar to mine. The idea motivated me to launch a company dedicated to helping women look and feel their best, beginning with their foundations.

I wrote a book about bra fitting, which became a bestseller. The book shared an approach to bra fitting that dared to reject the common practice of using a mathematical formula for calculating bra size. Eventually, my company began to provide bra fit training based on a methodology I created. The methodology became the basis of an online certification program in bra fitting for lingerie professionals. To my surprise and delight, the company ended up going global, with clients on six continents.

In my mind, the training we provided was so much more than fitting technique. It was the art of customer experience. I believed transformational fittings would guide women to shift their relationships with their bodies. I had glorious visions of retail stores around the world being places where women would come back, again and again, to tap into positive feelings and self-celebration.

It didn't work out quite that way.

My clients became amazing bra fitters, but most of them stayed narrowly focused on the technical procedure for fitting. They knew their work in the fitting room was emotional for women, but the majority of them didn't take the next step to incorporate the emotion intentionally in their business processes. As a result, they didn't maximize customer relationships, and my bigger vision for customer experience wasn't being fully realized.

One day, one of my clients told me her customers were literally crying tears of joy in the store's fitting room. The owner, her customers, and the employees were thrilled.

"That's great!" I said, genuinely enthusiastic about her success. Then curiosity struck me, and I asked, "Now, what are you doing to convert these happy customers into loyal buyers for the long term?"

She looked at me for a long moment, saying nothing. Then she opened her mouth, but no words came out. She stared at me in confusion and then said, "I offer great fittings, just like you taught me."

It never occurred to her that she would need to do more to secure long-term customers. In her mind, fittings were the job, so successful fittings would lead naturally to customer loyalty. She assumed happy customers would buy again.

I knew differently. From my years of experience working for large corporations, I knew companies needed consistent systems to cultivate long-term customer loyalty.

The lightbulb clicked on.

I started working with her to apply my customer loyalty know-how to her company. To improve the overall customer experience at her retail store, we:

- Crafted an authentic experience that made customers feel appreciated by the company.
- Illuminated internal company messaging about goals so all the employees were aligned with the company's priorities.
- Quantified customers' lifetime value and identified groups of customers who were most profitable.
- Aimed advertising and marketing messages toward those high-value customers.
- Expanded the relationship beyond the physical store so customers also felt appreciated when they weren't there, which triggered even deeper long-term loyalty.
- Celebrated customers, which set my client apart from her competitors.
- Trained the team consistently so they were on board with the company's loyalty initiatives.
- Analyzed key metrics to track initiatives for continuous long-term improvement.

These changes produced immediate results. Within a couple of weeks, one customer set the store's all-time record for spending in a single transaction. A couple of months later, my client hit her highest revenue month. She followed it up with a record-setting year.

When I used these techniques with other clients, they saw great results, too. The value of their average customer shot up. Customer referral rates skyrocketed. My clients were thrilled as their revenue gains accelerated. Many of them recouped their investment in my services within a few months, before we even finished their project. Plus, those revenue streams created long-term value that continued to generate returns years later.

I expanded my approach from my lingerie store clients to other areas of retail and then to companies and nonprofits involved in media, manufacturing, technology, healthcare, financial services, and more. My clients have included pre-revenue start-ups, single-person businesses, and multinational corporations.

My strategies have been implemented successfully at the executive leadership level, at divisional and departmental levels, and in micro businesses with a single leader. My approach to customer loyalty has also been applied by cross-functional teams for special projects and initiatives within companies.

Using my process, clients have gotten results.

One of my clients reshaped a sales conversation so that customers more easily understood her company's suite of products. Instead of buying just one thing, customers were now purchasing more items across several product categories; this was achieved simply by changing the way she introduced new products into the conversation. This small shift meant the upsell didn't feel like a money grab at the end of the transaction because the whole offer was integrated. Without spending a dime, the company added 4 percent to its revenue in the first year alone.

Another client found a better way to manage customer-facing communication in one department. With a small investment in technology, the company improved internal efficiency, cutting costs by one hundred thousand dollars per year. Plus, they found uses for the technology throughout the organization, compounding the savings without additional spending. This investment made the organization more efficient and extended employee tenure because a chunk of annoying, repetitive work was automated, freeing people up to focus on higher value work.

In other cases, my clients:

- Boosted average customer value by more than 96 percent.
- Improved email click-through rates by 167 percent.
- Upped the lifetime value of loyal customers by 29 percent.

One of my clients gained so much freedom and happiness at work after she implemented my process to boost customer loyalty, she swore it saved her marriage.

Cultivating loyalty is a process of implementing clear and consistent action across your organization. This book guides you through the process to keep your customers. Part I examines why loyalty matters for customer retention and the upside your company gets when you activate loyalty. Part II shows you how to identify and engage your highest-value customers. Part III teaches you the steps you need to take to retain those high-value customers for the long term. Part IV explains how to set up your company internally to make customer-facing initiatives a success. Part V walks you through the tactical steps to take action. How you implement the process will depend on your company's unique needs. You may already have some of the pieces in place. Your opportunity is to find the best way to put it all together for your business environment.

Change doesn't happen overnight. As customers interact with your new approach to customer experience, they'll feel seen, heard, and valued. You'll inspire customers to stay longer, spend more, and refer new business to you. When your customers believe your company values them, they'll want more, which means better results for you, your employees, and the people you serve.

PART I

Loyalty Is Lucrative

When loyalty is genuine and cultivated strategically, customers engage for the long term and become highly profitable. What is loyalty? In this book, "loyalty" refers to customers who care about their relationship with your company.

Loyal customers are a small subset of your overall customer base. Their value vastly exceeds their numbers. When you create a system to keep your customers, your company reaps the benefits today and into the future.

CHAPTER 1

Why Loyalty Matters

Think about your best customers. Now consider the system you have in place to attract, nurture, and promote your relationships with them. If you improved your system for cultivating loyalty, what would happen?

Loyal customers generally exhibit three key traits:

- They stay with your company longer.
- These long-term customers become highly profitable users of your products and services.
- Put the right system in place, and loyal customers also refer additional business to you and become your advocates.

Those three advantages—staying longer, spending more, and referring new customers—mean that loyal customers are highly valuable to your company. Since most companies have limited time and resources to apply to strategic projects, it's important to find ways to ensure your loyalty efforts produce profitable results.

In my experience working with a wide variety of companies, the juice you'll get from focusing on customer loyalty is definitely worth the squeeze. The benefits of cultivating customer loyalty are wide-ranging, producing financial returns, competitive advantage, and better employee engagement.

Loyalty Generates Financial Returns

Recent research into the financial impact of top customers has quantified the value of loyalty, and the numbers are jaw-droppingly compelling.

Historically, companies have applied the Pareto Principle to sales revenue. In this application, the Pareto Principle, also known as the 80/20 Rule, says 20 percent of a company's customers generate 80 percent of its revenue. That's a tall order. Does the rule stand up to scrutiny?

A 2017 study examined customer behavior at consumer-packaged goods companies. On average, the companies in the study generated 73 percent of the revenue from the top 20 percent of their customers. The 80/20 Rule wasn't fully realized, but it was close.

In another study, Dan McCarthy, a professor at Emory University, and Russell Winer, New York University, looked at product and service companies in a variety of industries that had consumer and business customers. In 2017, the companies generated a combined $4.3 trillion in revenue. The top 20 percent of these companies' customers delivered an average of 67 percent of their revenue.

While the 80/20 Rule might not precisely hold true, the findings are clear and consistent: whether it's consumer-packaged goods or other products and services companies, top customers deliver a hefty percentage of a company's revenue.

Top Customers Deliver Profits

Here's where it gets interesting. McCarthy and Winer also researched the profitability of top customers. They found the top 20 percent of those same companies' customers generated 105 percent to 113 percent of net income.

You might wonder how a subset of customers could be worth more than 100 percent of net income. It's possible because not every customer is profitable. The customers who are highly profitable compensate for the customers who are served at a loss.

The top 20 percent of a company's customers generate 105 percent to 113 percent of its net income.

In addition to being more profitable, it's less expensive to keep your top customer than acquire new ones. The Harvard Business Review found that it costs five to twenty-five times more for companies to secure a new customer versus retain an existing one. An ongoing cycle of new customer acquisition costs more than keeping the customers you've already won. It makes financial sense to make existing customers happy.

The power of customer retention is amplified when considering research from Bain & Co., which shows that when companies improve their customer retention rate by as little as 5 percent, they see an increase in profit of 25 percent to 95 percent. In other words, if you motivate just 5 percent more of your customers to stick with you, your profits can jump considerably.

Top customers are ultra-valuable, so it would make sense that companies make every effort to keep them loyal, yet I consistently see companies forfeit time, energy, money, and goodwill by neglecting the impact of loyalty. When companies shortchange loyalty, they shortchange their financial results.

Loyalty Boosts Competitive Advantage

In addition to financial rewards, loyalty boosts competitive advantage by repelling your competition. When customers are dedicated to your company, they're satisfied with the solutions you provide. That makes them less likely to consider your competitors.

For example, right now, I'm happy with a product that manages my company's customer database. I'm sure there are competitors. Maybe they're better or less expensive. But I'm not looking because I like what I have. The interface and functionality do everything I want. Every time I've had a problem, my current provider has solved it efficiently. I'm loyal. When someone asked me recently to recommend a company for this product, I gave my provider a full-throated endorsement.

Referral is one of the three identifiers of loyalty. Loyal customers tell their friends, family, colleagues, and even strangers about their positive experiences with your company. These referrals are high value.

Research shows that people trust positive feedback from people they know and even from strangers more than they trust reviews from experts, so referrals from loyal customers carry real weight on your behalf. These referrals are more likely to inspire action.

Loyal customers multiply their value by referring new business. One loyal customer's impact includes their individual spending and the cumulative value of every person they refer to your company.

Customers will talk about your company, but loyal customers aren't the only ones who will share their experiences. Unhappy customers also tell friends, family, and colleagues about their bad experience with your company. Their commentary has a negative impact on your potential customers. If that's not bad enough, unhappy customers tend to tell more people about their experiences than satisfied customers.

Social media magnifies those complaints. In the 1980s, studies showed that dissatisfied customers told nine to fifteen people about their bad experience. Sometimes, they told as many as twenty. Today, a company can only hope that negative word-of-mouth reaches a mere twenty additional people. When the average Facebook user has 338 friends and a viral complaint can reach millions, companies ignore word-of-mouth at their peril.

Once you've lost a customer, it's hard to win them back. Growth gets harder. Your cost of customer acquisition can skyrocket. Clearly, that's not efficient. In fact, quite the opposite: it's expensive.

Retain your customers and put an end to the hamster wheel of constantly having to attract new ones just to keep your existing level of revenue.

If loyalty means you can spend less and extract more value from your marketing compared with your competitors, that's another advantage. It's easier to be efficient with your marketing spend if you target the right people.

Before you can nurture a loyal customer, you have to attract a prospect to buy from you. Prospects become customers after they purchase your product or service for the first time. Knowing your most valuable customers' characteristics enables you to pinpoint prospects who fit a similar profile. That means you'll be able to speak to those high-potential prospects more clearly, which is more effective and also an advantage.

A clear, targeted marketing opportunity provides better results than a marketing campaign that goes out with a broader message.

The better you understand the prospects who are most likely to become loyal, the more you can leverage that marketing advantage.

Your company's advantage stems from knowing your loyal customers well enough to develop targeted marketing messages, product updates, and relationship-building opportunities.

Mark Suster is an entrepreneur and managing partner at Los Angeles-based venture capital firm Upfront Ventures. Upfront is the largest venture capital firm in Southern California, with more than $1.8 billion in total funds raised. The firm has backed such successful companies as Ring and Bird scooters. Suster says relationship building is one of the most misunderstood and important factors that business leaders get wrong.

"We don't celebrate the importance of engagement as a core skill set," Suster says. "It's a lot easier for people to stay in their comfort zones. Part of it is laziness. Part of it is fear. Part is not understanding the importance of loyalty. But loyalty has a profound impact on the products companies offer when they actually understand customers and their needs."

The better you know your customers, the more you can engage in ways that motivate deeper levels of engagement.

When I worked at a television network, our audience skewed toward kids and senior viewers, but the top brass wanted us to capture the more profitable demographic in the middle, the eighteen-to forty-nine-year-olds. Our marketing department was constantly pulled between targeting the viewers who actually watched the network and those people our executives wished were watching. We wasted a lot of money chasing people who were unlikely to become viewers, rather than focusing on people who fit the profile of our existing, dedicated audience members. Instead of trying to serve a wider array of viewers, we could have created deeper relationships with the people who were predisposed to become loyal to the network.

Loyalty Improves Employee Engagement

Customer loyalty may be primarily externally focused, but it also provides an opportunity to rally your employees and improve their engagement. Employees are integral to your customer loyalty efforts. When you inspire employees to embrace your customer loyalty goals, there is a benefit for everyone: employees, leaders, and customers. Engaged employees are another advantage for your company.

Employees who feel their contribution is valued are more inclined to feel connected to your company's goals. By 2025, 75 percent of the workforce will be comprised of Millennials and Gen Z. These employees didn't invent the concept of work that has purpose, but they're more vocal about expecting it. They need their work to matter. One way to engage them is to develop processes that show how they are making a difference for customers.

Employees who see how their work drives to a purpose that goes beyond profit are more likely to feel connected and engaged. Motivated employees who see sincere meaning in cultivating long-term customers will become invested in your loyalty initiatives. Some of my clients use their dedication to customer loyalty as a value that helps employee recruitment and retention, creating even more strategic advantage for the company.

Employees are a vital part of your customer loyalty effort because they're on the front lines of your company. In companies with face-to-face contact, employees engage directly with customers. But even in companies where customer interaction is virtual or through a distributor, customer experience can be designed with your employees in mind. When employees feel like valued contributors to your customer-facing initiatives, they become more invested in your company's success. Engaged employees help you activate customer loyalty.

Jackie Reses leads Square Capital, a division of financial technology company Square. Square Capital has extended more than $3.5 billion in cash advances and loans to more than two hundred thousand businesses. When it comes to the interactions between companies and their employees, Reses sees companies shortchanging relationships.

"Many companies provide lip service to the importance of loyalty. And they don't focus. They almost treat people issues as secondary," Reses says. "What I see is that companies don't always apply structured business decision-making to relationships in the same way that they would other business issues. They don't value it because it feels like a 'soft side' issue to them, and I don't think it is. If leaders really applied business rigor to people issues, they would get better results."

Will This Help You?

The companies that benefit most from implementing a system for customer loyalty generally fall into three categories in terms of their relationships with their customers.

- Your company is experiencing high customer turnover, and you want to stop the bleeding.
- Your company attracts customers, but their enthusiasm is lackluster. You want to increase the lifetime value of your existing customers.
- Your customer turnover is low, and customers keep buying. Your company is looking for new ways to grow.

If any of these statements sound like where your company is today, you will benefit from getting serious about customer loyalty. My experience and research have established that a consistent, well-executed process for customer loyalty will improve profits, provide a competitive advantage, and boost employee engagement across any industry. In the coming chapters, you'll learn the strategy and tactics to guide you to successfully keep your customers.

CHAPTER 2

The Five Factors That Unlock Loyalty

Loyalty isn't just a philosophical construct, it's a dynamic practice of ongoing interaction with customers. Your company cultivates long-term customer loyalty by applying five key factors to customer engagement on a consistent basis. These are the five factors that unlock customer loyalty for your company.

Factor 1: Prioritize Emotional Connection with Customers

You boost loyalty when customers feel connected to your company. Their sense of connection develops when customers feel seen, heard, and valued. Seen, heard, and valued are three distinct components that lead to loyalty.

Customers feel seen when you interact with them as individuals, when your company recognizes what they do throughout the duration of their interactions with you. They believe their actions are noticed.

My husband is a car fanatic. For many years, he was a dedicated BMW guy. He wore BMW gear, attended BMW events, and raced spec BMWs. One year he went to Germany to pick up his car in person before shipping it home. Then he purchased his fifth BMW—and nothing happened. Even though he'd been a member of the BMW club and registered every car with the company, he got no recognition for his loyalty. No swag. No card. Not even an email that acknowledged his purchases. It was a missed opportunity for the brand because a little attention would have cemented his loyalty for life. Instead, he didn't feel seen. His next car was not a BMW.

Customers feel heard when their voice matters. Whether they have a complaint or compliment and whether they speak to the company directly or via other public channels, customers feel heard when they're authentically acknowledged for sharing their thoughts. I say, "authentically" because an automated email with a generic message doesn't register as acknowledgement. You can automate a reply, but your effort to convey sincere appreciation goes a long way.

Social media makes it easier and harder to hear your customers and respond. It's easier because a tweet that mentions your company can be tracked and flagged for a fast response. It's harder because it takes more resources to set up and monitor the changing landscape of social media networks. For smaller companies, social media can feel overwhelming. Yet missing out on one customer's interaction can make a lot of customers feel ignored and, by extension, not heard. Customers who don't feel heard are less likely to become loyal.

Customers who feel valued believe a company cares about more than merely the money they spend. When a company's behavior leads customers to sense that their patronage matters, they feel valued.

Zappos is legendary for its customer service. The company makes it a priority in words and actions inside the company. Their customer service message is part of everything from interviewing recruits to training employees. The message is applied to customer interaction across the brand. Zappos CEO Tony Hsieh even wrote a book about customer happiness. Zappos knits its mission to "wow" customers into the fabric of the company, and employees are authorized to take action to make customers feel valued. Stories abound about Zappos shipping shoes overnight free of charge or allowing customers to keep shoes, gratis, that were shipped in error. One Zappos employee even got on a plane to personally deliver fine jewelry that belonged to a customer and was accidentally shipped to the company along with returned merchandise.

When customers feel seen, heard, and valued, they get invested in their relationship with your company. The feeling of seen, heard, and valued is a vital component of successfully cultivating loyalty, but it's not the sole factor for success. That's why emotional connection is only the first factor for loyalty.

When customers feel seen, heard, and valued, they get invested in their relationship with your company.

If you take away nothing else from this book, remember the intention to make customers feel seen, heard, and valued as a foundation for customer interaction.

That said, intention is not sufficient for success. It's not enough to understand the idea of emotional connection that invites customers into a relationship where they feel seen, heard, and valued by your company. Success will be rooted in the way you apply connection throughout your company. You need a clear process for consistent action to make emotional connection a viable and profitable reality. That's why emotional connection is only the first factor for loyalty. The remaining factors get into the strategy and tactics of implementing your customer loyalty initiative.

Factor 2: Create a Process with Clear Goals

Your message of connection comes to life in your company when it's paired with a systematic process. The feeling of being seen, heard, and valued has to be translated into specific goals so your employees understand their role in the process. Begin by establishing clear goals for everyone in your company to achieve. Specific goals enable employees to unite behind achievable outcomes.

Creating goals isn't the super-sexy part of cultivating loyalty. Measurable goals aren't exactly swoon worthy. Yet your specificity in setting goals ensures your employees are in sync, marching toward a single destination.

A good specific goal is one that a) your employees clearly understand and b) is the right objective for this moment in your company. Good specific goals help employees know exactly what they're trying to achieve and define how they'll know when they've successfully accomplished the goal.

No matter how big or small your company is, or even if you're a sole proprietor, creating clearly articulated goals is an important part of cultivating loyalty. In addition to helping you clarify priorities, specific goals help you explain your priorities to your team. In the world of loyalty, your team is anyone whose work impacts any aspect of your customer's experience, whether directly or indirectly. Even if you don't have employees, you still have vendors, agencies, freelancers, and other partners who are on your team. Your entire team needs to be aligned to optimize customer loyalty.

Factor 3: Break Your Goals into Measurable Steps

Not only do you need a goal that everyone understands, but you also need to make sure people know how that goal applies to their unique role in your company. If your team doesn't know what they're supposed to do next or how to do it, even the most inspirational goal is unlikely to be achieved.

Well-defined goals lead to measurable steps that begin with your current reality and end with your objective being met. Completing a series of clearly defined, bite-sized tasks is how your company moves to the finish line. Customer loyalty requires active participation. At every level of your organization, your team should know exactly how they are supposed to contribute to the goal. To get everyone on board, you need to provide loyalty-driven tasks and hold employees accountable for completing them.

Invite employees into your vision for better customer relationships. Give them a way to be successful with customer interaction, complete with information, training, and sufficient support for their efforts. These activities require time, energy, and effort so your team of employees and partners can be successful with your customers.

Factor 4: Apply Tracking and Metrics

You can't measure your process without data. Cultivating loyalty requires tools to track and measure progress. Once you have those tools in place, you'll need to find a way to gather the data you've collected and analyze it so you can learn and improve.

Factor 5: Add Celebration

Celebration happens when you mark moments of excellence with activities that notice and reward those moments. Celebration comes in a variety of forms. You can reward customers for their interaction with you. You can celebrate employees for reaching customer goals. Celebration brings creativity and fun to your company. When it's done right, celebration is a great way to give people a sense of your company's values. The more people feel connected to your company, the more they will be inclined toward loyalty.

Celebration for loyalty is distinctive because it's applied systematically. As you align your company for loyalty, you'll identify ways to consistently add celebration to your customer loyalty efforts.

Some companies skip this step or celebrate customers on an ad hoc basis. Sometimes those one-off celebrations can be brilliant. An ad hoc approach might work in a tiny business with a single owner who's responsible for most customer interaction, but that's not a sustainable system. Even if you don't have employees, a systematic approach that incorporates celebration reflects a company that's oriented toward future growth.

Balance Connection and Data Using the Five Factors

These five factors are woven into every aspect of customer loyalty. Some of these factors focus on building connection with customers. Others are driven more by rigorous application of process and data. Some business leaders are more inclined toward connection while others prefer process and data. To keep your customers, your company needs all five factors, incorporating both connection and process.

Kara Nortman co-founded Moonfrye, a children's e-commerce company, and incubated what became Tinder at media company IAC. Today, she's a partner at venture capital firm Upfront Ventures.

"I work with CEOs, some of whom have started companies before, some of whom it's their first time," Nortman says. "Some of them I have to push to become more data-driven. They're too oriented toward feeling and instinct. Others are too data-driven. I need to push them toward art and storytelling. I have to encourage them to take risks."

Regardless of your personal preference, customer loyalty requires both emotion and rational thinking. You'll need to make these components equally vital parts of your successful customer loyalty initiative, even if they aren't equally comfortable for you.

Why Doesn't Everyone Cultivate Loyalty?

Given the financial, competitive, and cultural advantages of customer loyalty, it would seem like a no-brainer that companies would emphasize keeping their customers.

I see a lot of organizations that prioritize new client acquisition. New clients are vital to any company. But customer retention can be challenging when companies focus too much on customer acquisition and fail to invest in customers after they buy.

Companies emphasize efforts to sell to new customers, rather than retain existing customers, in part because selling to a new customer is easier to track. It's binary. You didn't have the customer, and now you do. It's simple to attribute the sale to a specific moment. You can ring a bell, bang a gong, or send a company-wide email to mark that moment. That definitiveness is appealing.

Once a customer comes on board, there are many points of interaction with your company. It's harder to identify exactly how, when, or who is responsible if those interactions go well or poorly. Since a customer's decision to buy again (or not) after the initial sale can be attributed to multiple departments, companies tend to drift toward the easier path of focusing on new sales rather than retention and upselling efforts.

Another reason companies prioritize efforts to sell to new customers is that in many companies, salespeople are the rainmakers. Because the sales role is, de facto, tied to money, a lot of companies have cultures that revere sales. These companies invest in their sales talent, and the "sales guys" are the big shots. Even if a company's leaders don't have sales experience, an executive can be brought in as the "big gun" to close a deal, reinforcing the notion that sales to new customers are the organization's most important activity. This approach is especially apparent when companies talk about "sales" and "revenue" as if they are synonymous. Using those terms interchangeably suggests that customer acquisition is the only revenue driver. In fact, the greatest value in a customer's contribution comes after the first sale.

Some companies discount ongoing customer interaction because they believe it's enough to deliver good products and services. These companies can miss opportunities to cultivate loyalty at the deepest and most profitable levels.

Restaurants are a great example. Many, if not most, rely on good food and service to bring customers back. They don't extend the customer relationship beyond the meal they're serving at the moment. By missing out on opportunities to reengage and remind customers of their good experience, restaurants lose opportunities to boost revenue.

What I often hear from business leaders is some version of, "Customer retention is everybody's responsibility." On some level, that's true, but it misses a fundamental reality: a job that belongs to everybody belongs to nobody. Customer loyalty is inherently cross-functional. It needs a point person who can enforce your ongoing initiative and help your people succeed across multiple departments.

Ultimately, people are at the heart of loyalty. People want and need to feel appreciated. Advances in technology don't eliminate this fundamental human characteristic. In fact, quite the opposite. When you build connections with people you serve, your customers feel appreciated and become invested in their relationship with your company. They care about being your customers, and they believe you care about them.

This is a critical distinction. It implies a relationship is a two-way street between your company and your customers. Your relationship with them and theirs with you is what drives the financial, competitive, and cultural advantages that come with deeper customer loyalty.

Not every company is willing to focus on relationships. Some companies would rather drive transactions. I once worked with a large online apparel retailer. The company's repeat purchase rate was low, and they wanted to improve it. We audited their customer experience and discovered their website was guiding buyers to the wrong products for their needs. This misdirection explained why so many customers purchased once, returned what they bought, and never purchased again.

This discovery was an opportunity. By connecting customers with the right products for their needs, the company could generate loyalty, reduce churn, and improve long-term customer value. I identified a few ways the company could accomplish this specific goal. The change seemed straightforward to me, and I was excited for them since the upside potential was tens of millions of dollars annually.

I was surprised when the CEO said, "I don't care if customers are buying the wrong products so long as they're buying." A company that doesn't care if customers buy the wrong products and never buy again as a result won't successfully cultivate loyalty. This company chose not to change its approach. Instead, it continued to spend a lot of money to attract and churn through a parade of one-time customers.

I see a similar dynamic in some start-ups, especially venture capital-backed start-ups. These companies are often so focused on fast growth and a big exit that they don't emphasize the actions that motivate long-term customer value. Mark Suster and I agree that this is short-term thinking.

"Building a great business comes down to having a brand that customers love," Suster says. "A brand isn't built on marketing campaigns. It's built on customers. The problem with scaling so quickly that you disappoint customers is that you can't rebuild trust. Companies that undermine customers' trust rarely return to greatness."

When companies launch, they can focus so much on building their product or service and trying to get customers to buy that they don't consider the experience customers will have once they come on board. That's a missed opportunity. A company's highest-value customers can be some of the earliest buyers. Getting early customer relationships right has a big financial upside for start-ups.

In life and in business, relationships take effort. Cultivating loyalty requires time and attention. It may require investments in people, processes, and technology as ingredients for long-term growth.

Every company takes a slightly different approach to cultivating loyalty.

I've created an online resource to help you identify your opportunity with real outcomes for long-term loyalty. Get this and other free resources here:

www.keepyourcustomersbook.com/resources

PART II

Target Your Most Lucrative Customers

Your plan to keep your customers begins by digging into the subset who have the most potential for deep and deeply profitable loyalty. Discovering who these customers are, where to find them, and how to engage them are your first steps to keeping them loyal.

CHAPTER 3

Pinpoint Your Loyal Customers

C ultivating loyalty begins with defining your best customers, the people who love what your company offers and are most inclined to engage in a long-term affiliation. You'll want to keep a clear picture of these customers in mind when you create your loyalty initiatives.

Upfront Ventures' Nortman says, "Look for customers who see you as one of the top three brands in their world. When they wake up in the morning, these are the brands they turn to in their jobs or lives. Those are the customers you want. Companies have to ask, 'Who are those people? How do we find them? How do we make them feel loved? How do we get real insight and feedback so they feel heard? How do we communicate so they understand us? How can we make them feel like part of our decision-making process?'"

Companies are often quick to say, "We have lots of loyal customers," and that may be true. However, it's important to distinguish between different flavors of loyalty. Loyal customers are not all created equal.

There are three distinct kinds of loyal customers. Each has its own characteristics that you must understand so you can find the group who will see your company as one of the top brands in their lives.

---

*Loyal customers are **not** all created equal.*

Lucrative Loyals

Sought-after customers who are emotionally connected to your company are your "lucrative loyals." Lucrative loyals are ultra-dedicated. They:

- Buy consistently and are highly profitable.
- Feel a genuine connection when you earn their loyalty.
- Care about their experience as customers.
- Engage by referring prospective customers.
- Provide testimonials and communicate inside and outside your business, such as via social media.

Your goal is to identify your lucrative loyals because your company will get its best returns when you focus your energy and attention on them.

You speak to your lucrative loyals by tailoring your programs, product design, marketing, and other outreach to their wants and needs. When you're clear about your lucrative loyals' profile, you can target similar prospective customers for acquisition. Your company has the opportunity to provide a strong, clear message about who you are and why you're worthy of their money. The more you craft the messages you put into the marketplace to address your lucrative loyals, the better your chances are to attract and retain these customers.

Lucrative loyals are often confused with other customers who display characteristics of loyalty but aren't actually lucrative loyals. These other groups are limited loyals and lazy loyals.

Limited Loyals

Limited loyals are moderately invested in their relationship with you, primarily because a threshold exists for them to exit. Limited loyals may be long-term repeat customers, but they lack engagement and connection. They may not even like the company that has earned their loyalty.

Why do customers continue to buy from companies they don't like? Perhaps there's a switching cost, a barrier to exit, or no better alternative.

In the travel industry, some loyalty incentives are alluring. Once you have achieved a certain status with a hotel chain or airline, the rewards can be compelling. Upgrades are sweet and sticky.

Nortman says, "I don't really care about my hotel rooms, especially for business trips. Since I travel a lot, I tend to use the same hotel company over and over and now I have status. Status gives me rewards, which keep me coming back. I'm not loyal to the hotel chain. I'm loyal to its loyalty program."

Software-as-a-service makes it hard for customers to leave. Consider customer relationship management (CRM) software. A CRM system contains a lot of important data. Invariably, CRM companies make it easier to put the data in than to get it out. Exporting data to a new system is generally complex and painful. Those barriers to exit mean companies retain customers because the pain of leaving isn't worth the gain.

Banks are a similar case. You can close your existing account at one bank and open a new account at another bank, but it's hard to find the moment when that's the best use of your time. The hassle of opening the new account, moving your money, ordering new checks, moving direct deposits, and setting up autopayments is annoying. Banks know this, and they retain a lot of limited loyals as a result.

Companies might be able to attract folks who will become limited loyals with marketing campaigns. And those customers might end up staying for the long term. But if they don't feel emotionally connected, their loyalty is limited.

Lazy Loyals

Lazy loyals are repeat customers who buy from you on a transactional basis. They buy repeatedly purely out of convenience. They don't have any real sense of loyalty to your company compared with your competitors. You're just the easy choice. These customers are loyal in a sense, but they'll leave you without a backward glance.

When I lived in New York City, every workday I walked past several sidewalk coffee carts between my subway stop and my office. They all sold the same bagels and croissants. The coffee was equally mediocre. Yet I always stopped at the same cart to buy my morning coffee. I had my guy, and I felt loyal to him—right up until the day I left that job and my commute changed. I never went back and never cared. My loyalty was lazy. It was convenience and nothing more.

Lazy loyalty exists in many sectors for many reasons. Any customer who buys repeatedly simply because it's easy is probably a lazy loyal. There's nothing wrong with these customers, and there's only upside to treating them well. Enjoy your lazy loyals, but don't waste your resources to attract more. Lazy loyals will find you when it's convenient for them, and they'll leave whenever they're ready to go.

Lazy loyals don't buy from you because of your great marketing. Directing marketing toward others who share their characteristics is unlikely to provide good returns. No matter how fantastic your campaign is, they won't stick with you once their circumstances change. There's no business advantage to spending your limited resources to market to them when there's so much more to gain by focusing on your lucrative loyals.

In most companies, the majority of customers are average. An unexpectedly high number at any given company are probably one-time buyers.

Research by Zodiac Metrics revealed that "for pretty much every company that we have seen, even those having what are considered 'incredibly loyal' customers, 50-80% of customers transact once and never come back."

Zodiac didn't look just at repurchase rates within a certain time period, they looked at repurchase rates according to the specific buying cycle of the industries they studied. For example, the cycle for purchasing milk is very different from the cycle of purchasing a new car. Even taking those purchase cycles into account, the story stays the same. The biggest chunk of your customer base will be average. Even among your loyals, the lucrative segment likely will be smaller than your lazy or limited loyals. Given how valuable lucrative loyals are, you'll want to clearly identify them as quickly as possible.

Lucrative Loyals Drive Revenue

Some business leaders have concerns about aiming their efforts toward lucrative loyals. These leaders worry that by serving a single, relatively small group of customers they will antagonize or alienate others. "What about our other customers?" they ask. "Don't we need to worry about them, too?"

The answer is yes and no.

Focusing on lucrative loyals doesn't mean you should belittle any other customer segment. Every customer deserves a great experience, and anyone who pays you should be treated with respect. Once you antagonize or alienate customers, they will speak poorly about you. Negative word-of-mouth is an expensive mistake. Unhappy customers can produce "anti-referrals" that keep other high-value prospects away.

Limited loyals and lazy loyals will stay with you as long as it's convenient for them. There's not a lot you can do to keep them if they're customers of convenience—unless your customer experience motivates them to upgrade.

A customer who begins a relationship with your company as a limited loyal or lazy loyal might eventually fall in love with your company. When companies deliver an excellent customer experience, it's easier for customers to choose a higher level of loyalty. A thoughtful system for cultivating loyalty lets customers choose more. The lazy and limited can become lucrative. The key is designing a customer experience for lucrative loyals that's well-executed and sufficiently inviting.

When you aim your customer experience toward your lucrative loyals, you'll still attract other customers. Targeting your marketing, messaging, and customer experience to your lucrative loyals doesn't mean you're turning away other customers.

Consider a Hollywood blockbuster summer action movie. Movie studios know most of their raving repeat viewers are teenaged boys and young adult men. Those groups are most likely to be the lucrative loyals for these movies. Knowing that, studios skew the movies and marketing toward teenaged boys and young men. But they aren't the only fans of action movies. Just because the studios focus on making movies that young males love doesn't mean other moviegoers will have a bad experience.

Look to the Future

Lucrative loyals aren't just valuable today. An investment in relationships with these customers is an investment in the future of your company.

When you can quantify a customer's value across their former and future interactions, it helps you identify the investment you can reasonably make to acquire that customer. It can be smart to spend more to acquire a future lucrative loyal, rather than save a little yet net a lazy loyal or limited loyal. The better you know your lucrative loyals' characteristics, the easier it will be to decide how much to invest in acquiring new customers.

Lucrative loyals are high-value customers, in part, because they appreciate feeling a connection to your company. The more connected they feel, the more they'll invest in their relationship with you. When you build your customer experience to cultivate long-term loyalty, you build a relationship that develops bonds between the company and customer over time. The more lucrative loyals feel seen, heard, and valued, the more their loyalty is reinforced. It's a virtuous cycle.

You have an opportunity to learn what motivates your loyal customers to choose your business again and again. When you create a process that taps into those motivations, you have an opportunity to influence their actions in the future.

An orientation toward long-term customers will shift how you engage with your lucrative loyals. When you see a relationship as long-term, you interact differently to build a foundation of trust.

In business terms, you focus more on the benefits of repeat purchases and less on maximizing the immediate sale.

Another reason lucrative loyals offer so much value is their multiplier effect. When you look at your overall relationships with your lucrative loyals, it's important to see the whole picture. Lucrative loyals are worth more to your company than the amounts they spend. One of their traits is they love telling other people about you. They tell their friends, colleagues, and strangers how much they love your company. Those referrals can inspire folks to buy from you as well. When that happens, the lucrative loyal's overall value to you increases.

Identifying Your Lucrative Loyals

So, you're looking for your lucrative loyals. Great! Now, how do you find them?

Begin with data that helps you understand individual customer's purchase history. When you can tie spending to individual customers, you can find your lucrative loyals. Key metrics include purchase amount, frequency, and interaction throughout the relationship with your customers.

Start with the low-hanging fruit: repeat buyers. Beginning with customers who've purchased more than once is a simple and effective way to narrow your population of potential lucrative loyal customers.

Ultimately, you're looking for ways to quantify each customer's overall value to your company, and financial contribution is one important measure of that value. The better you can identify a customer's long-term value, the better you can categorize him or her as a loyal customer. Even if those customers spent less at first, your goal is the more profitable long-term relationship, not the short-term transaction.

I worked with a wellness company whose profile of lucrative loyal clients included the characteristic of signing up for a package of ongoing care services instead of buying a la carte. Once clients transitioned to the ongoing care model, their long-term value jumped more than tenfold. Those customers made more appointments, stayed for a longer duration of care, and generated more referrals. These customers were vastly more profitable than those who purchased services separately. The more customers used the business, the more likely they were to become lucrative loyals. Knowing that to be the case, the company priced the first upgrade from a la carte services to a package in a way that made the package a no-brainer from a cost perspective.

Next, track referrals. It's not always easy to know when a customer makes a referral, but it's always in your best interest to understand when that happens. This is especially true when the referral results in new business. Since lucrative loyals feel connected to your company, they're more likely to refer other people to your business. Find ways to identify referrals whenever possible. This can be easier in some companies than others. Referral codes and other online tools help customers make referrals and help you catalog them. For companies that don't use those methods, there are other creative ways to provide incentive to customers to make their referrals known.

Some of my clients send a gift when customers make referrals. This process requires the companies to create a habit of asking new customers if they were referred. When a referral is identified, the company sends a thank you gift to the customer. Customers who are inclined toward lucrative loyalty quickly catch on to this gifting bonus. Referrals go up and so does the company's ability to track them. Tracking referrals can be as much art as science, but it's worth the effort because any customer who has referred business to you is more likely to be a lucrative loyal.

A third opportunity to identify lucrative loyals is to capture customer interaction. Part of lucrative loyalty is a greater inclination to build a deeper relationship via interaction with your company, so it's valuable to have a process for tracking customer engagement. Identify where your lucrative loyals are most inclined to engage. Online, this might be social media platforms, like Facebook or Twitter. Yelp for businesses that cater to consumers (B2C) and any number of industry-specific sites for businesses that provide services to other businesses (B2B) are additional areas for customer engagement. You should also monitor internal customer support channels, such as service calls, email, and technical support tickets. Even when customers call to complain, they're engaging with your company. Another way to examine engagement is to track which customers open your emails, click through your emails, or use promotional codes you generate.

As you dig into your customer base, you'll be able to identify a frequency of engagement that determines your set of lucrative loyals. Once you understand who these customers are, it's time to activate their emotional connection with your company through a consistent, systematic process to reinforce that connection.

CHAPTER 4

Activate Customers' Connection to Your Company

Tapping into positive feelings generates real business advantages. When you create experiences in which customers feel consistently seen, heard, and valued, you win lucrative loyals. When people sense they are truly appreciated as customers, it triggers the emotional connection associated with highly profitable loyalty.

This is true for companies of all kinds, whether they're B2C or B2B. In the world of customer loyalty, this distinction fades away because no matter who your company sells to, all companies sell to people, and people are wired for connection.

Connection and loyalty aren't strictly logical endeavors. There's some emotional component involved in purchase decisions. This emotion extends to customer behavior. In fact, research by McKinsey & Co has shown that 70 percent of a buying decision is based on how people feel in their interaction with you. The feelings drive the purchase. The *Journal of Marketing Research* also found that brands that inspire higher levels of emotional intensity receive three times more word-of-mouth recommendation compared with less emotionally connected brands. That emotional intensity translates into new customers and additional revenue.

UrbanStems is an online flower delivery company that focuses on creating a better gifting experience. Co-Founders Ajay Kori and Jeff Sheely are dedicated to creating happiness across every aspect of their company. They found their company's emotional connection with customers in an unexpected way.

"We started UrbanStems thinking we'd focus on making it easier for guys to send flowers to the women in their lives," Kori told me. "We got it wrong. What we found is that the majority of flower senders are women. Guys send [flowers] when they have to, but women send when they want to, and women send a lot more often for everyday occasions. Our best customers are the kinds of people who will share something they grow obsessed with, and with the experience we deliver, they get obsessed with us."

Find the Heart and Smart of Loyalty

Some business leaders are uncomfortable tapping into emotion as a way to generate and grow their business. They pride themselves on being data-driven and believe rational decisions are best, so they shy away from the notion of emotion in business. If business leaders see emotions as "mushy" and mushy as bad, then anything that smacks of mushy can't possibly be good business. These leaders miss out on opportunities when they steer their company to ignore the emotional connection of loyalty, because data alone doesn't win loyal customers.

Other business leaders are so focused on creating an authentic connection with their customers that they resist any effort to create consistent processes. They see data as constraining and prefer to engage "organically" with their customers. This approach also sells loyalty short. Data provides rich customer information that can be used strategically to deepen connection. When it comes to loyalty, it's not an either/or decision. Cultivating lucrative loyals depends on leaning into both emotional connection and data-driven analysis.

Companies that cultivate loyalty successfully begin by defining the emotional connection for their unique group of lucrative loyals. Companies discover what makes those loyal customers feel appreciated by the company. They determine how to create the emotional connectedness that makes those customers feel seen, heard, and valued. This is the heart of loyalty.

The smart of loyalty occurs when companies weave emotional connection into a consistent, systematic process for engagement that can be tracked, measured, and assessed.

Cultivating lucrative loyals depends on leaning into both emotional connection and data-driven analysis.

Successful orientation for lucrative loyalty requires heart and smart. The outcome is loyal customers who want to buy, buy again, and tell their friends.

If your company misses the heart of loyalty, you won't have customers who feel invested in your company's progress. Plenty of people have wallets full of rewards cards for stores to which they feel no loyalty at all. These companies might track the data of customer interactions, but there's no emotional connection. Without that, customers don't feel compelled to share the company's products and services with friends. They don't refer colleagues.

If your company misses the smart of loyalty, you'll end up with a random array of customer interactions. Some interactions may activate loyalty, but others won't, and you'll never know the difference. If you don't know what is or isn't working, it's impossible to learn or grow. You'll make the same mistakes over and over again. You'll miss the nuggets of customer gold that could reinforce loyalty and become huge money multipliers.

To be clear, focusing on emotional connection doesn't mean constantly giving in to customers' demands. Nor does it mean changing who you are to serve the whims of customers' desires. In fact, quite the opposite. Emotional connection includes being crystal clear about what you do and how you engage. It means managing expectations by drawing boundaries at the outset of your customer relationships and then authorizing your team to enforce those boundaries. Clarity frees you to be generous with your company's emotional connections within those boundaries so you can focus on inspiring consistent loyalty with your best customers—your lucrative loyals.

Convert Customers to Lucrative Loyals

The path to cultivate loyalty and convert customers into lucrative loyals is activated through a customer's experience with your company. Your company will foster loyalty most successfully when you tailor customer experience to your lucrative loyals.

Companies have a variety of departments that provide some kind of customer support. These departments can have different names, such as customer service or customer success. Each department has distinct functions in a company and deals with specific aspects of customer interaction.

Customer experience is not a department. Instead, it's the sum of every point of interaction between a customer and a company. Customer experience includes customer support functions as well as departments like sales, marketing, and more. Customer experience includes every aspect of a customer's perception of, and interaction with, a brand.

Customer experience is not a department. It's the sum of every point of interaction between a customer and a company.

A customer's experience begins the first time he or she hears about your company, whether through a marketing message, word-of-mouth, or direct interaction. The customer experience continues through every step of their lifespan as a customer to the last follow-up interaction. How your company manages its customers' experience will distinguish you from your competitors. In the ideal scenario, customer experience is a series of interactions that consistently activates heart and smart so that customers feel they are seen, heard, and valued.

If customer experience is defined as less than the sum total of a customer's interaction with a company, it suggests that the customer's experience is the task of only one department. That does a disservice to both the customer and the company. Cultivating loyalty depends on every person in your company being actively engaged in elevating customer experience.

My husband and I stayed at Hotel Erwin in Santa Monica, California, for our tenth wedding anniversary. I booked our stay through a third-party website and soon after received an email from the hotel asking whether we were staying for any particular reason. I replied and shared that we were staying for our anniversary. A couple of months later, we arrived at the hotel. When we checked in, the front desk attendant congratulated us on our celebration. When we got to our room, we found a bottle of Prosecco in a fresh bucket of ice, along with a lovely anniversary card.

Consider the mechanisms that connected those dots. The hotel sent the (likely automated) email, asking for information about the reason we were visiting. They took the time to read our email and add the key data to our profile. The information popped up to remind the front desk to congratulate us as we checked in. Housekeeping was notified to put the bubbly in our room so it was waiting for us yet still icy cold when we arrived.

Across the hotel, people in several departments took the information that had been captured and converted it into actions that made us feel appreciated. This is how companies activate heart and smart.

The Role of Customer Experience

Customers have always had experiences, but the art and science of customer experience as a business discipline is relatively new. As customer experience becomes increasingly recognized as a powerful opportunity to attract, serve, and retain customers, more companies focus on getting customer experience right.

The definition of customer experience varies from company to company. Sometimes customer experience is confused with customer-facing functions that are tasked with different subsets of customer experience. These functions include customer service and customer success.

Customer service is probably the more familiar of customer-facing functions. Everyone has contacted customer service at some point, whether by phone, email, or online chat. Customer service is the group that aids customers when they request help with support, repair, purchase, return, and other transactional needs. Customer service functions may change based on the company, but generally customer service resolves problems that customers bring to companies. Interactions are initiated by customers who reach out to companies for assistance, making customer service an important part of a customer's experience.

For example, at a newspaper, customer service fields phone calls from customers who want to order or cancel a subscription, didn't get their newspaper, received a wet paper, or need a vacation hold, among other issues. Interactions with customer service may not be complex, but they are important because they set the tone for engagement. Customers may call with relatively small frustrations. How customer service deals with those minor irritations can diffuse or escalate based on the quality of the interaction. Your customer service reps' guidelines, the amount of training they receive, and the ongoing management of the customer service team all contribute to the overall customer experience.

Customer success oversees a customer's usage of a company's product or service. This function tends to be associated with B2B companies that sell a relatively complex product or service that's set up after the point of purchase. When a company's products or services require expert help for implementation, that job falls to a customer success team. They ensure a new customer is able to integrate and use the product or service seamlessly.

A customer success team begins to work with a customer the moment a sale is made. After making a purchase, the customer success team shows that new customer how to use the product or service. This process can include technical elements, like making sure the purchased product integrates into a customer's existing technology environment. It can also include the training employees need to get the most value from the purchase. The process of getting a new customer up and running with their new purchase is called onboarding.

After onboarding, customer success generally manages ongoing customer interaction, regular check-ins, and sometimes renewal, upselling, and more. While customer success is often associated with the technology sector, it exists in other industries as well.

Consider Salesforce, which offers a suite of B2B technology-based products that make customers more effective. When someone buys one of Salesforce's products, it's not a one-and-done sale. The buyer is likely to need help integrating the new products into their existing technology environment. Employees at the buyer's company need training to use the products and often have questions that require additional support to ensure ongoing use. Executives will likely want to understand how the product is being used effectively. All of this might mean a buyer's employees need help to use their Salesforce purchase. Without that help, the buyer might not fully integrate Salesforce. They won't get the value of their purchase and could end up discontinuing their subscription to their suite of Salesforce products. To avoid that outcome, Salesforce engages its customer success folks to manage some aspects of the company's customer experience.

Your company's relationship with a customer might begin with a marketing initiative or direct outreach from your sales team. Your customer service department might help customers with login or account problems or provide basic technical support. Customer success might focus on helping customers get the most benefit from the application and usage of your company's products and services. All of these functions fall under the umbrella of customer experience. But wait, there's more. Customer experience also includes:

- Aligning customer interaction with your company's strategic vision, mission, and values.
- Tying engagement to your company's visual branding to avoid brand confusion. You can negatively impact the customer experience if your visual branding is inconsistent. Any time customers are confused about your brand, consciously or subconsciously, it can erode trust.
- Managing customer communication from various departments in your company. A well-intentioned company might have employees from sales, marketing, customer success, and other functions all reaching out to customers. Without a clear, company-wide process, you can end up with message inconsistency, which is another barrier to loyalty. If too many team members try to engage at one time, they might over-communicate. Even when it's well-intentioned, over-communication can overwhelm and annoy customers.
- Sending the right communication for customers' needs in a timely way. One of my clients sent all of its onboarding materials to new customers at the moment of purchase and didn't follow up after that initial data dump. The company's intention was good. The team's objective was to make sure customers had everything they needed to use the product immediately after purchase. But it was too much, too soon. Customers missed the value of the information when it was sent, and then forgot where to find the infor-

mation when they needed it later. Once identified, the problem was simple to fix so the company could provide a better onboarding experience for its customers.

Walker, a customer experience consulting firm, estimates that customer experience will overtake price and product as the key differentiator for brands in 2020. Gartner is one of the world's leading research and advisory companies. Their latest study of customer experience reveals that it's the new marketing battlefront. According to a recent Gartner Customer Experience in Marketing survey, more than two-thirds of marketers said their company competed mostly on the basis of customer experience, and 81 percent said they expected to be competing mostly or completely on the basis of customer experience within the next two years.

Investing in Loyalty Pays Off

Your process for heart and smart is what drives the particular way your company sees, hears, and values your customers. Creating that emotional connection will take time and effort. It often demands an outlay of money as well. Some companies need to invest in people, process, and technology. Others need to invest in understanding their customers so they can deliver connection to those who are (or might become) lucrative loyals. Fortunately, the investment pays off fairly quickly.

Retail business owner Cheryl Cote added a cloud-based inventory management system to her company, Esprit de la Femme. Understanding her best customers inspired her to shift inventory selection, customer outreach, and marketing messages. Within ninety days, she tied her investment to financial returns that turned into consistent, double-digit growth at a time when brick-and-mortar retail had seen tough times as an industry.

David Simnick, CEO of Soapbox, invested in market research to design a profile of his ideal customers. The insights that came from this research led directly to a 250 percent growth in sales.

Esprit de la Femme and Soapbox are just two companies that have experienced the benefits of successfully cultivating loyalty. We'll learn more about their stories later.

CHAPTER 5

Create a Bullseye and Aim for It

Cultivating loyalty is a team effort. It requires the people inside your company to be on the same page for customer experience. To achieve synchronicity, you will benefit from a singular articulation guiding everyone's activities.

That singular articulation means customers experience consistency from their first interaction with your company. Companies often struggle to find this message, and a misstep can get your customer relationship off on the wrong foot. If a customer's first experience with you is messy, it undermines their trust in the relationship. Once trust is damaged, it's hard to recover, and it's harder for customers to feel seen, heard, and valued. To get your company into alignment, you need a goal for customer experience that everyone can aim for, together.

Aim for the Bullseye

The way to drive consistency and coordination is to have everyone in your company directed toward the same target. The center of the target is where you win the most points, so to cultivate lucrative loyals, you want your organization to aim for the bullseye.

Your bullseye is a specific kind of message for customer experience. It's an internal message that gives your people a focal point. The bullseye message must be shared by every person who works for your company.

By being both a catchphrase and rallying point, your bullseye message helps your team aim and re-aim. The bullseye is a reminder of a company's core promise to its customers. It is also a beacon that lights the path for action by your team. The bullseye message underscores your company's unique expression of seen, heard, and valued.

The bullseye is a reminder of a company's core promise to customers and underscores your company's unique expression of seen, heard, and valued.

Your bullseye is not the same as your mission.

Companies often create foundational purpose statements of their mission, vision, and values. Sometimes these strategic guideposts have other names, such as North Star or Rules of the Road. Whatever they're called, they're crafted messages for the outside world about who you are as a company. When these statements are relevant and used consistently, they can be valuable, but they have inherent drawbacks as guideposts for customer loyalty.

A bullseye isn't a strategic vision. It's a working premise for customers. It's a phrase that guides decision-making for your team. A bullseye is specifically designed to be a day-to-day foundation for boots-on-the-ground action with customers. It guides employee interaction throughout a customer's experience.

A bullseye message must be accessible. It must be something that everyone in the organization can understand and that employees can use as a target for execution. For this reason, customer loyalty aims for the bullseye.

A classic example of a customer loyalty bullseye is "the customer is always right." Let's say a company has "the customer is always right" as their bullseye message. All the employees know that "the customer is always right" is the best guide for customer interaction. When the company's leadership says the bullseye is "the customer is always right," your team has something concrete to guide their engagement with customers. It gives employees something they can use reliably.

Is "the customer is always right" the best bullseye message for your company? Probably not, and here's why: when it comes down to daily interaction, most companies aren't willing to make the concessions to customer demands that reinforce turning that messages into reality. They're unwilling to put their money where their mouth is. Even the legendary Nordstrom had to change their "customer is always right" return policy because it no longer made business sense for the company. If the bullseye isn't a true guide for employee action, then it won't work in your customer experience process. But I use "the customer is always right" as an example because it's a recognizable bullseye that's simple, easily repeated, and a message everyone can aim toward in customer interactions. That's the benefit of a bullseye.

Since it functions as a message to guide internal behavior, a bullseye often differs from a slogan or tagline, which is an external marketing message. Apple's tagline, "Think Different," doesn't define the customer relationship. In fact, while Apple creates great products and provides good service in its stores and through technical support, the company does very little to reach out to its customers and engage for loyalty. Apple's customer bullseye could be, "We're here for you."

Zappos' tagline has historically been "Powered by Service," and their mission is "To Live and Deliver WOW." These both align with their customer orientation, so Zappos is a company whose bullseye is strongly aligned with its mission and tagline.

Make Sure Your Bullseye Fits

Your bullseye message is a simple phrase that applies to your philosophy for customers in any given situation. Occasionally, if rarely, a bullseye message evolves organically in a company. Most companies find their bullseye through a formal process, such as a bullseye workshop, that leads them through a series of steps to arrive at a message that's distinctive and meaningful for them.

Your articulation of the bullseye message is important, but how you use the message effectively is far more vital to successfully cultivating loyalty. Companies have to make sure that the message—once identified—will work as an active guide for employee behavior.

A bullseye message does more than guide customer interaction. It guides the entire customer experience. It can even help remind you which customers you're aiming for, and that can prevent your company from going after the wrong customers.

One of my clients was a small manufacturing company that had brought on a new customer a few years before working with me. This customer was not just big for my client but a huge player in the industry my client served. When the customer approached my client, they were ecstatic. They saw themselves as being called up to the major league.

As part of the deal, the customer wanted my client to develop a specific line of new products. To produce these products, my client invested in research and development, paid for design, and purchased new manufacturing technology. Despite these required investments, the future for the partnership seemed bright. After the first run of the product came off the manufacturing line, the customer came back to my client. They still wanted the product but at a fraction of the price. My client balked, but the customer held firm.

My client had a choice to either continue manufacturing the product for pennies or say no and lose their investment. Since this product was outside their expertise, they didn't know whether they could recoup their investment with other customers.

Their big customer pressed them to make a decision quickly. In desperation, they took the deal, and it almost destroyed them. By diverting resources to serve this one customer, they were unable to serve their existing customers with the same level of quality and attention. They lost long-term customers who were paying higher prices. Their profitable business lines deteriorated. By the time they came to me, their revenue was 80 percent lower than it had been, in large part because of the Faustian deal they'd made serving one big fish.

Clarify Who You Are First

Had my client focused first on a bullseye, they could have done a better job of assessing the risks of taking on this big customer.

They were so dazzled by the customer's name, they lost sight of themselves and their goals.

After working with me, their bullseye message became "less is more." The company took a streamlined approach to its products and customer experience. "Less is more" governed everything from vendor interviews to customer service. They were not a luxury brand, so "less is more" meant identifying a few important moments of customer interaction and concentrating on making those moments special. The company leaders created protocols to guide the customer team's communication of the "less is more" message. Their bullseye influenced product development by helping them converge on an internal agreement to offer a core suite of products to companies they could serve with excellence.

If this company had the bullseye in place when the big fish came knocking, it would have clarified their decision-making process. Sadly, missing their bullseye was a multi-million-dollar lesson for this company. In the aftermath, they emerged ready to guide the company back to growth.

Find Your Bullseye

To find your bullseye, identify the emotions your products and services evoke for your customers, and then use that emotion to form your message. The process to develop a bullseye looks at different levels of connection between your customers and your company, using the concentric rings of a bullseye target as a guide. The rings start with the largest and work toward the smallest, which is your company's heart and bullseye message.

Your bullseye includes:
- Company fundamentals.
- Features and benefits.
- Value.

- Personal improvement.
- Emotional driver.
- Bullseye message.

The outermost ring includes the non-negotiable aspects of your company. Anything that is a fundamental principle of who you are and what you do goes into that outer ring. Your mission, vision, and values statements, if they exist and are actively relevant, go here. Also in this ring are the products and services your company offers and a clear picture of your lucrative loyals. When you add all of these together, you develop a solid foundation for who you are as a company.

The next ring includes the features and benefits that make your products and services the best solutions for your customers' problems. These are points that differentiate your products from your competitors'.

Features and benefits are similar but distinct components of your offerings. A feature is an aspect of your product or service that differentiates you from your competitors. For example, a feature for a home builder might be standardized use of thicker insulation throughout the houses they build. The benefit is that thicker insulation makes a home more energy efficient.

Consider how your products' features and benefits provide value for your customers. In other words, why should your customers care about those features and benefits? More specifically, how do those features and benefits improve your lucrative loyals' purchases? How are they helpful? The homebuilding company uses thicker insulation (the feature), which makes its houses more energy efficient (the benefit), which saves money for its home buyers (the value).

The next ring focuses on ways your company's products and services provide personal improvement for its customers. It's the first point at which you begin to incorporate emotion into the process. Consider the emotional connection between your lucrative loyals and your company. Ask yourself, "How does our company make the lives of our lucrative loyals better?"

"Better" is subjective and tied to the characteristics of your lucrative loyals. A homebuilder's customers might feel loyal to a variety of differentiators. Some might value energy efficiency so they can afford their monthly bills. Others might value lower energy costs so they can save more for their kids' college education. There's no right or wrong; there's only knowing the preferences of your lucrative loyals. Knowing what your lucrative loyals value most makes it easier to identify the triggers that inspire their loyalty.

The penultimate ring encircles your bullseye. In this ring, there is a single emotional driver that captures the upside your customers get from the cumulative outer rings. Home buyers might feel "safe" when they can afford their monthly bills. They might feel "freedom" by having more money for retirement. The homebuilding company has to determine which emotional connection drives its lucrative loyals.

Knowing how your lucrative loyals feel when they're best served by your company completes the outer rings of your bullseye. That information serves as a guide to your bullseye and a message that captures the products and services, features and benefits, value, personal improvement, and key emotion of your company. A builder whose lucrative loyals want to feel financially free to have more money for retirement might have a bullseye of "we've got this." This message conveys a caring, long-term relationship with customers that suggests a high level of service.

The bullseye process is the same for B2C and B2B companies. All companies have an opportunity to identify a fundamental emotional connection that speaks to their lucrative loyals and then use it to express a unique bullseye message.

Customer engagement has to start with who you are. When you reverse the steps, you can end up defining yourself according to your customers, instead of the other way around. Without a clear guiding principle that provides a foundation for your company, it's hard to build. Instead, you'll sway with any movement from your customers. Building your company on your customer's vision for who you are is quicksand, and it's deadly.

Having a bullseye also helps you define priorities for decision-making by providing a strategic focal point. When an alluring opportunity comes along, your bullseye becomes an objective perspective that can temper excitement in the heat of the moment. Your bullseye reminds you which kinds of customers fit your lucrative loyal profile, so when big fish come calling, you have objective criteria on hand to assess the opportunity. It's always easier to do that analysis when you've created those criteria in advance. Otherwise, it's too easy to be momentarily dazzled.

Of course, it's important to listen to key customers. That's what cultivating loyalty is all about. At some point, a company may choose to add or change products and services for a customer's needs. But the first step, creating your bullseye, has to come from within. Once you have that message, you're ready to use that bullseye to target your lucrative loyals. Create the foundation for the company you want to build and then tailor it to the people who are most inclined to be long-term loyal and lucrative customers.

Knit the Bullseye into Your Company

Once you have your bullseye message, make sure it's drilled into every facet of your company. Coming up with a bullseye isn't enough to make it take root. Repetition and reinforcement nurture the bullseye so that it's knit into the fabric of a company. When every part of the customer's experience is guided by a singular aim, it creates consistency. Consistency begets trust, and trust is a necessary ingredient for cultivating loyalty.

Consider the bullseye as a guide for customer communication. You may never use the words in your bullseye message for marketing, but the spirit of your bullseye should infuse the language you use to talk to customers. For my manufacturing client, the words "less is more" were never used as a marketing slogan, but the underlying orientation was used as a guide that infused my client's marketing messages. The company's advertising and trade show booths were spare but striking. The customer experience always tied back to that foundational principle. This was achieved by making sure the bullseye message was integrated throughout the company.

Embed the bullseye message into your team with a training protocol that extends beyond the initial announcement. Ritz-Carlton is legendary for its approach to customer service. New employees are formally trained in the company's approach to customer service excellence before their functional job training begins. After that, each shift begins with an employee lesson about one of the company's pillars of excellence. This training keeps the ongoing emphasis on excellence front and center.

To make your bullseye truly come to life, team members will need to use it consistently to guide customer interaction. This takes repetition over time. You want it to become so engrained in your team that it's second nature. You can't overshare your bullseye.

For this reason, it's beneficial to craft a bullseye that can become a mantra for the inner workings of your company. And like a mantra, your bullseye is designed to be repeated. When used effectively, bullseyes are part of the DNA of a company's customer experience efforts.

The bullseye message guides employees to make small and large decisions. Any time a team member is doing something customer-facing, the bullseye should be their guide for decision-making.

The bullseye guides your team across a wide array of activities inside your company. For example, if your team is working on a website update, they can use the bullseye as a guide. Do the decisions for design and language underscore the message of the bullseye? Are they speaking to the heart of your lucrative loyals? Are all the features in sync, using aligned language and tone? Consider every touchpoint, down to the personalization of your artificial intelligence chatbot for customer support and investigate ways to improve alignment with your bullseye.

Consistency improves your opportunity for meaningful customer relationships, and any inconsistency damages that connection. The same is true for every aspect of customer interaction. From sales and marketing to human resources, the way you communicate about your company is based on a working proposition that you can use to align your messaging.

Your bullseye.

It's not enough to create a bullseye. It must be regularly activated within a company to be effective. Companies achieve consistency when leaders continuously reinforce the importance of the message in both word and action and when they use it to drive customer experience. They highlight ways the bullseye enhances loyalty so team members see the value of its application. Using your bullseye message habitually helps everyone in your company aim for loyalty.

The magic of your bullseye will be found in a clear voice driven by a strong vision for the customer's experience. Once you have your bullseye message, it needs to be reinforced.

Then reinforced again.

And again.

When you are clear and consistent, your company's bullseye message will be the foundation for every step of a customer's journey to loyalty.

CASE STUDY: CLUSTERTRUCK

Chris Baggott is the CEO of ClusterTruck, a delivery-only restaurant with a menu inspired by street food. Customers use an app or go online to order food. The food is prepared with local ingredients inside a single kitchen owned by ClusterTruck. Everything is made from scratch. Sauces are made daily.

The timing of food preparation ensures that everything is finished at the same time. The hot food is hot. The cold food is cold. Nothing wilts under the death glare of a heat lamp. As soon as an order is completed, ClusterTruck takes the food from their own kitchen to their own drivers who deliver the food quickly and efficiently. The company controls every aspect of the customer experience, from menu design to food preparation to delivery.

Baggott brings a rare skillset to ClusterTruck. In addition to being a farmer and restaurant owner, he is also a tech guy. Chris was the co-founder of ExactTarget, a cloud-based marketing solution that was sold to Salesforce in 2013 for $2.5 billion.

ClusterTruck isn't merely a food prep and delivery system. Like ExactTarget, the company has a sophisticated technology back end that distinguishes it from its competitors.

"What struck me as we were getting into this business," Baggott says, "was looking at the third-party delivery apps, which were primarily our competitors. This industry has very high consumer dissatisfaction, yet insatiable demand. Nobody is happy with the solution, but they want it. They want their problem of prepared food delivery solved, and they're willing to suffer through bad food, poor quality, long waits, and surly drivers. We set out to solve all of that with one solution."

Because ClusterTruck controls everything from food sourcing to putting deliveries in the hands of their customers, the company is able to provide a much better experience for customers.

ClusterTruck's customer experience is guided by a bullseye that seems simple: "don't ship maybes."

What's a maybe?

"Don't ship maybes" began as an instruction to the kitchen staff about approving orders before sending them to the drivers for delivery. If an order got through food production but the meal wasn't perfect, employees were trained not to send it out. Instead of sending out a so-so meal, they remade the order. In other words, don't ship a meal that's a maybe.

Over time, "don't ship maybes" became a guidepost that expanded beyond the kitchens of ClusterTruck. The expectation is excellence, and the guiding principle is clear. When everyone in a company is focused on their part of the customer's experience, excellence is the result. And a culture where every interaction is designed for excellence is a great breeding ground for loyalty.

Baggott is so dedicated to ClusterTruck's bullseye that it has literally become part of his DNA. He tattooed his arm with a reminder: "don't ship maybes."

If "don't ship maybes" applied only to the quality of their food orders, it would be a great bullseye for the kitchen. And that's all it would be.

But Baggott didn't stop with that narrow definition. He wasn't satisfied with stopping at the kitchen door. He sees "don't ship maybes" as something bigger, more all-encompassing. By thinking more strategically about the phrase, he made "don't ship maybes" a bullseye for the entire company.

Talking to a new food vendor? Take the time to ensure they're the right partner for ClusterTruck. Look beyond the food to their philosophy. Determine whether they will align with ClusterTruck's dedication to local, high-quality ingredients. "Don't ship maybes."

Hiring a new employee? It's better for the company to wait for the best candidate instead of filling a position with a warm body for the sake of short-term ease. Find the best person for the job. "Don't ship maybes."

"'Don't ship maybes' is any food that isn't perfect," Baggott says. "It's any experience that isn't perfect. It's not hiring the right people. It's our core mantra—no maybes."

Chris has used the mantra of "no maybes" for continuous improvement to the customer experience at ClusterTruck.

Knowing customers' food preferences has helped the company identify menu additions, deletions, and changes that have improved the customer experience.

Baggott added, "We did an analysis of our three best-selling items: the breakfast burrito, taco salad, and what we call the bowl-rito, which is basically a burrito with no shell. Then we started digging deeper, asking, 'What are the modifiers for each item?'

"With the breakfast burrito, the number one modifier is no bacon. Taco salad, it's no meat added. Bowl-rito, it's no meat added. We realized we were selling our top three items to vegetarians. That informed our menu. We said, let's introduce more vegetarian and vegan options. Let's modify some existing menu items to be vegetarian and vegan. Avocado toast always came with an egg. We lowered the price, took the egg off, and made the egg an add-on. Now when people sort the menu by 'vegan,' the avocado toast pops up.

"The old way, if a menu item had an egg on it, the customer could remove the egg, but because we don't reduce prices when people remove ingredients, customers ended up paying for something they didn't want. So we made those changes and customer satisfaction and reorder rates went up."

In other words, making customers pay for something they didn't want was a maybe. Making vegetarians and vegan customers work harder to find options to match their needs was a maybe.

Having "don't ship maybes" as a bullseye has paid off for ClusterTruck. In the restaurant business, an average restaurant sells $300 to $600 per square foot. Cheesecake Factory, which is legendary for its profitability in the restaurant world, sells around $1,000 per square foot. ClusterTruck sells about $1,600 per square foot.

Chris created a bullseye for excellence and became the champion for "don't ship maybes." By aligning his company to "no maybes," he defined the tone for the fundamental premise and promise of ClusterTruck. That's what a clear bullseye can do for your company.

CHAPTER 6

Calculate the Lifetime Value of Your Loyal Customers

With your bullseye in place, you know exactly what guides your customers' experience. Everyone in your company aims together toward loyalty. Now it's time to use your bullseye to create a tailored customer experience that speaks to the heart of your lucrative loyals.

Venture capitalist Kara Nortman says, "Find your most loyal, most addicted customers. Then build a great, repeatable business winning them, serving them, and getting them to come back with a high rating versus going after a huge market where you're just okay."

To target your addicted customer base, you have to understand them as people. Your objective is to create marketing messages that resonate so clearly, your lucrative loyals think you're talking directly to them. When that happens, they feel seen, heard, and valued, and you get results. You reduce your cost to acquire a customer. There's a financial benefit to knowing how much to invest in targeting loyalty. Being able to quantify customer value makes it easier to build a strong business case for new programs and initiatives that target your lucrative loyals.

The Value of Loyalty

It turns out, you can put a price on loyalty. Quantifying the value of your lucrative loyals can be simple or complex, depending on your company's needs. I've helped companies that kept their customer files on paper index cards, and I've helped companies with sophisticated systems for compiling customer data. Yet, every company found a way to improve their process to identify and target loyal customers. Some needed to upgrade their approach to customer data. Others needed to simplify and tailor the customer information they used. Your goal is to rightsize your insights into the value of your customer base for your company's needs.

You can put a price on loyalty.

Companies often look at the amount of money each customer has contributed in the past to determine whether he or she is a best customer, but when companies look only at past revenue or net income contribution, they can misidentify their best customers.

Several elements contribute to the whole picture of a customer's significance to your company. That complete picture is quantified by:

- Customer lifetime value.
- Referrals.
- Engagement.

Calculate Customer Lifetime Value

Customer lifetime value is the sum total of a customer's spending with your company, from first dollar to last. Customer lifetime value is a forward-looking metric because it looks at past data and projects future spending. It allows companies to quantify a customer's entire span of spending, not just what he or she has already purchased.

To understand a customer's lifetime contribution, actual past spending information is solid data that provides clues to the future, but it's not foolproof. Past spending fails to capture the entire customer relationship.

Your biggest customers today might not have the greatest customer lifetime value. Consider my manufacturing client. They wanted to serve a big-fish customer, and it backfired spectacularly to the point of sending their revenue into freefall. On the other hand, a small customer may spend less today, yet if you cultivate their loyalty, they may ultimately stay with you longer and buy more over time. That customer can become more valuable to your company than the customer who comes in, buys big, and leaves. Similarly, a dedicated customer who has bought a ton from your company in the past might look like a valuable customer to cultivate. But what happens if that customer moves its manufacturing overseas or your company's biggest vendor goes bankrupt?

Past behavior doesn't necessarily indicate future action.

To understand a customer's overall contribution, companies need a way to predict and quantify their customers' future value. Fortunately, there's a way to look forward at a customer's overall significance by calculating customer lifetime value.

I like Peter Fader's approach to customer lifetime value. Fader is a marketing professor at the Wharton School, where his expertise centers on the analysis of behavioral data to understand customers. He's the author of Customer Centricity: Focus on the Right Customers for Strategic Advantage. Fader also happens to be one of my favorite professors from Wharton, and I credit him with sparking my first interest in long-term customer value. Somehow, his class managed to make grocery store scanner data compelling.

"We're seeing that customer lifetime value can be a game-changer," Fader says. "Its use cases are growing, and it has the ability to bridge silos, offering a 'gold standard metric' that everyone from marketers, research and development people, human resources, and senior executives can share." When customer lifetime value is used effectively across organizations, it provides a way for many departments to unite around the importance of a customer's contribution.

Customer lifetime value adds up the total contribution of each customer so you can determine the overall worth to your company. You calculate customer lifetime value by looking at:

- A customer's average sale amount.
- The number of additional sales you expect from them.
- How long you expect to keep them as a customer.
- The profit margin associated with their purchases.

You can calculate customer lifetime value by revenue instead of profit margin. You can also factor in the cost of acquiring a new customer to help you decide how much you're willing to invest toward that objective. The math is simple once you have a process to accurately assess the future-looking component.

Any predictive analytic involves both art and science. The key to pinpointing your customers' future actions is being honest with yourself about how much they're actually likely to spend, not just how much you hope they'll spend.

For example, many lingerie retailers say women should replace their bras every six months and then try to build their customer lifetime value calculations on the assumption that customers purchase bras twice each year. Lingerie retailers can't accurately predict future purchases by applying the twice-yearly standard. In reality, customers tend to replace their bras every couple of years. Many go much longer between purchases. Lucrative loyals generally buy much more frequently.

While past behavior is an important component of customer lifetime value, your ability to accurately predict a customer's future actions is where customer lifetime value shows its magic. That's why it's important to know your customers. The better you know them, the more accurately you can predict their behavior and quantify how their relationship with your company will evolve. In the lingerie world, one of the best predictors of a lucrative loyal is how quickly a customer purchases more bras.

Referral Extends Customer Value

There's more to customer loyalty than customer lifetime value or spending alone. Referrals add another layer to overall customer value.

When you inspire customers to become lucrative loyals, they tell other people how much they love your company. They don't merely refer others to you. They shout your praises to the rafters. They drag their friends to your door. They pull out their laptops and show folks your goods and services. They gush about their experience in spontaneous testimonials. All this positive word-of-mouth improves the likelihood of converting prospects into new customers.

These endorsements have real business value. The Nielsen Company's Global Trust in Advertising Survey says, "The most credible advertising comes straight from the people we know and trust. More than eight-in-10 global respondents (83%) say they completely or somewhat trust the recommendations of friends and family." The same report reveals that people are four times more likely to purchase when referred by a friend. Not only are they more likely to buy, but they're worth more to your business.

Research also reveals that the lifetime value for new referral customers is 16 percent higher than that of customers who came onboard without a referral. Referred customers begin their relationship with a higher level of trust, which translates into a higher lifetime value.

The impact of referrals applies to both B2C and B2B companies. Indeed, 84 percent of business-to-business decision makers start their buying process with a referral. To streamline decision-making, people rely more heavily on information from their personal networks, which means the power of referrals is stronger than ever.

Referrals are also a key identifier of lucrative loyals. The willingness to actively refer others to a business is a trademark characteristic of a lucrative loyal.

When calculating customer lifetime value, a company should take into consideration the value of new customers that an existing customer brings to the business. If an existing customer refers a new customer, it makes sense to credit the new customer's spending to the existing customer's value. You wouldn't have your new customer without the old one.

The secret to capturing the value of referral is to credit customers appropriately in your customer relationship management software. Your customer tracking system has to attribute the new, referred customer's purchases to the original referring customer.

There isn't a foolproof way to capture, track, and measure every referral, but companies are finding methods to connect the dots between referrer and referred customers. There are high-tech ways to identify referrals, such as providing codes that activate benefits to existing customers when they refer new purchasers. There's also nothing wrong with asking new customers if they were referred to your company, provided your team captures that information and applies it to your customer database.

Engagement Is Part of Customer Value

Engagement happens whenever a customer interacts with your company. Engagement can include social media, chats with customer support, and more. Loyal customers are highly engaged. That's why engagement is part of customer value.

One way to track engagement is by making note of any direct interaction with your internal customer support teams, such as customer service or customer success. Simply identify the number of times a customer reaches out to your company. Every touchpoint has value. It's also valuable to track negative interactions, such as complaints. This is especially true if a complaint is resolved quickly and to the customer's benefit.

Any time a customer speaks about your company in a public forum, such as through social media, you can capture that as engagement data.

Personas Paint the Picture of Your Lucrative Loyals

As you refine the characteristics of your loyal customers, help everyone in your company aim for those buyers by creating a clear profile of those customers.

Companies often create profiles or personas that clearly articulate the characteristics of an ideal customer. To target loyalty, create a persona that's a detailed description of one person who represents a composite of your lucrative loyals. Companies condense the characteristics of their ideal customer into a single composite because it's easier to create marketing messages that are directed to a single person the persona represents.

Well-designed personas have enough specific information to make these ideal customers come to life. This makes marketing messages more resonant for the people you're trying to attract, your future lucrative loyals.

Developing business communication that resonates gets harder all the time. This is true in large part because we're all inundated with marketing messages. The American Marketing Association estimates that people are exposed to as many as ten thousand brand messages a day, and that number keeps growing.

Your company's communication has to cut through all of that noise. Your company's customer persona helps you create marketing that is specific and resonant. It makes your ideal prospects take notice. When you speak clearly to the right people using the right messages in the right setting, you can successfully convert customers faster and more effectively. That's what every business wants.

With a targeted approach, you can win over prospects quickly and efficiently. The more finely honed your communication, the easier it will be to find and convert high-value customers.

Big Results from Small Places

There is one other advantage to knowing your lucrative loyals' specific characteristics. Since people are bombarded with marketing messages, the more clearly your messages are crafted for your lucrative loyals, the more easily you can distinguish yourself from your competitors. When you're very clear about the characteristics of the customers you're targeting, you can be more efficient with your advertising dollars. Mass media channels for communication can mean you're paying to reach people who will never become your customers. You pay big dollars to communicate with a lot of people, when your actual value-per-prospect is low.

Conversely, when you are able to identify small media channels filled with people who are much more likely to be your target customer, your marketing spending can be much more effective. These small, targeted channels are called niche markets. The more you know about your lucrative loyals, the better you'll be able to identify your company's high-value niche markets. Going after the right niche markets is a solid strategy to attract new customers who are more likely to become future lucrative loyals.

When you know your target customers at a deep enough level, you can find the unusual places they might hang out. You can find them when they aren't expecting a marketing message from you. You can find them when they're more relaxed. A niche marketing strategy, when done properly, can be effective because it lets you talk to prospects when their guard is down, which further improves their receptiveness to your message.

The more you know about your lucrative loyals, the better you'll be able to identify your company's high-value niche markets.

When I worked at *Golf Digest*, our advertisers included golf equipment companies, golf destinations, golf clothing, and other golf-related businesses. We also had advertisers that sold financial advisory services, high-end liquor, watches, and cars. These non-golf-related companies targeted golfers as customers because golfers tended to be wealthy professionals who wanted and could afford upscale lifestyle brands. Plus, these advertisers knew that when golfers read *Golf Digest*, they were in leisure mode. They were in a good mood. Their guard was down. They would be in a better frame of mind to consume the goods and services that were being advertised. For those luxury advertisers, golf was a target-rich marketing niche.

Identifying the niche places where your prospective lucrative loyals spend time achieves that same result. The more granular your knowledge of these people, the more specific you can be with targeted messaging. Marketing to a niche allows you to be more efficient with your spending and achieve a better conversion rate. While each click or impression might cost more upfront, those clicks are more likely to convert at a higher rate, making them more cost effective in the long run. When you really know your targets and your niche strategy is on point, the return on your advertising investment can skyrocket.

The last key argument for using a niche strategy, or any customer experience strategy, is that you can demonstrate how well you know your prospects as people. You took the time to understand them. You speak to them where they like to be and in a language they understand. When you take the take the time to discover where your customers spend their time, they'll be more likely to feel seen, heard, and valued. When your customers intuit that you're talking to them in a place and manner that's tailored to them, you create an ideal environment for developing long-term customer relationships.

CASE STUDY: SOAPBOX

Soapbox is a consumer-packaged goods company. They sell soaps, shampoos, conditioners, and other personal care products. The company was founded with a strong social mission. For every product sold, Soapbox combats disease by donating a bar of soap to people in need around the world. The Soapbox slogan, "Soap = Hope," is emblazoned across everything the company puts into the marketplace.

"I wanted to improve clean water initiatives, so I decided to make soap," says David Simnick, CEO of Soapbox. "I literally started Soapbox in my kitchen. My express purpose of donating soap is to help reduce disease. We have worked with homeless shelters and food pantries in the United States, plus non-government organizations in sixty-five countries.

"We started selling in a couple of mom and pop stores and at farmers' markets. And then we got into Whole Foods and other stores that primarily sell natural and organic products, and then we got into Target. And we just kept going.

"Retail stores employ teams of buyers who decide which products will be sold to their customers. Buyers at Target, CVS, and Wal-Mart wanted to bring in a brand like Soapbox. Buyers were inspired by their ability to impact millions of people's lives and donate so many bars of soap.

"From the outside it seemed like, 'Oh my gosh, Soapbox is killin' it.' We were getting in a lot of stores. We got a lot of distribution through big commercial retailers. But it didn't matter. At a certain point, we were struggling.

"We found a cultural truth. We had been told by a bunch of people that if your differentiator is a social mission, your marketing needs to scream the social mission. In reality, we found out it's not enough to have a mission. Your product has to sell on its own merits. The social mission is just icing. The mission is what makes your products unique and different and so much more. Because you have that mission, you have that soul. And that soul, I believe, is a crucial element of winning in today's marketplace. Your soul has to be authentic. It has to be genuine. And we had that.

"Yet consumers weren't buying. Soapbox was on the verge of failing."

Soapbox got a lot right in the launch of their company:

- The company's social mission was meaningful, and they developed a network of partners on the back end to deliver the soap to people in need around the world.
- The company had the business acumen to get into both large and small retailers.
- The buyers at the big retailers loved them and backed them because having Soapbox meant they themselves were making a difference.
- The product was good.

Still, the company missed a key element, one that's necessary to build customer loyalty. With a little digging, the company discovered the problem: poorly designed packaging.

When prospective consumers stood in front of the shelves in a store, trying to decide what to buy, they glossed over the Soapbox products because the package wasn't visually appealing to them. The social mission was nice to have, but it didn't inspire prospects to pick up Soapbox and try it. In fact, the packaging prevented people from discovering the social mission because they never picked up the package at all. Prospects weren't being converted to customers.

"You have to excite and delight consumers to hit home," Simnick said. "A consumer doesn't buy just because you give back. She's not there to contribute to a charity. She's there to buy an amazing product. If you have an amazing product that looks phenomenal and is well priced, you check all the boxes *and* you give back; that's a different story."

No matter how good your product is, if no one is enticed to buy it, it's a failure. Your communication with your prospects has to be a two-way street. You make an offer, saying, "This is who we are," and the prospect responds by saying, "Yes, your offer speaks to me."

"Great brand building comes down to how you create emotional connection with the consumer," Simnick said. "We needed to do a better job understanding our key demographic and how we presented our product to her to make that connection. We needed to build affinity with consumers who would fall in love with our products and tell everyone within earshot about Soapbox.

"When we started the company, we didn't take the time to do that right. Honestly, we missed that step. We just didn't know any better. We never asked ourselves, 'What does our demographic really want?'"

To answer this question, Soapbox hired a marketing agency to aim the company's brand presentation and packaging to its prospective lucrative loyals.

Simnick said, "The research we did was about understanding our customers so Soapbox's products would call to them from the store shelves. We did a bunch of focus groups to better understand our key consumers. The theme that won was the idea of 'Thoughtfully Luxurious.' Then we created a product design that resonated with them."

Once new packaging was in place, customers felt Soapbox was talking to them. Sales went up, and once customers bought the product, they were more likely to be attracted to the company's social mission.

"It's actually interesting—because the study's results suggested our products could sell about 250 percent more with the packaging that won. We chose a design concept, and our growth number is pretty damned spot-on," Simnick said.

Soapbox's product was being lost to prospects until the company articulated which consumers it was targeting. The company homed in on what the right customers wanted and created a visual package that spoke to those people from store shelves. By establishing clearer communication that focused on prospective loyal customers, the company enjoyed a 250 percent increase in sales.

PART III

Use Your Customer Lifecycle to Build Loyalty

We've explored the philosophical foundation for loyalty, power of lucrative loyalty, and how to identify your unique set of loyals. Now we turn to tactics. Here's how to create a customer relationship that will be irresistible to your unique set of lucrative loyals:

- Welcome new customers into the world of your company.
- Onboard new customers to maximize loyalty.
- Emphasize inflection points throughout your customer's experience.
- Add rightsized celebration.
- Refine your tailored experience for lucrative loyals.

CHAPTER 7

Make a Positive First Impression to Jumpstart Loyalty

The moment a new customer decides to do business with your company is an important one. It may sound cliché to say, "You only have one chance to make a first impression," but clichés exist for a reason. In this case, not only is the saying true, but it also makes a crucial point. Sadly, a company's new customer welcome is an opportunity that's often overlooked. Make your welcome special. Let it be a moment that thoughtfully sets the tone for the relationship you want to build with your customers.

Companies that build their customer experience for long-term loyalty craft their welcome thoughtfully.

Your welcome should do two things. First, acknowledge your new customer's decision to choose your company. Your customer had options, and they picked you. Show customers you appreciate their decision. Second, share a clear expression of who you are and what you stand for as a company. The experience of being a customer is different from the experience of being a prospect. Your welcome should be a clear transition out of the sales conversation. It reinforces why your customer chose you and projects the care you have for their experience.

Take a moment to consider your own experience as a customer, whether as a business customer or consumer. Other than an automated email, how many times has an organization taken the time to acknowledge your initial decision to buy? How often did they make the outreach feel personal and authentic? How did that affect the initial launch of your relationship with that company?

Well-executed welcome programs are rare, which is great news for you.

The Benefits of a Welcome Program

Creating a process to welcome new customers is an opportunity that has several benefits. A well-crafted welcome program is memorable. It sets your company apart and stands out. The outreach and moment of connection will speak to the heart of those customers who are already inclined to become lucrative loyals. The welcome program also sets the tone for engagement with every customer. Loyalty, and even lucrative loyalty, is not preordained. Customers can choose to upgrade their interaction with your company based on how they feel. You can motivate customers to become lucrative loyals. A thoughtful welcome program is a great way to start a relationship that targets loyalty.

You can motivate customers to become lucrative loyals.

Your welcome program also demonstrates your commitment to making customers feel seen, heard, and valued. Since the welcome launches your relationship with your customers, a thoughtful approach is reassuring. It lets customers know the messages that lured them to buy weren't just snake oil. That moment is the first expression of what they can expect as a customer, so a good welcome improves your odds of keeping that customer. Your welcome shows there's consistency in the transition from prospect to customer. Consistency builds trust, and trust is a necessary ingredient for long-term loyalty.

Since a proper welcome is rare, a well-designed welcome program will differentiate your company from your competitors. Even if they have some kind of welcome program, when you connect your welcome to the expression of your brand and the clarity that comes from your bullseye, your welcome will naturally be differentiated from anyone else's.

Create a Welcome That Launches Loyalty

A welcome that wows begins with your bullseye, so start with that message in mind. You're embarking on a relationship. Like any relationship, when you clearly convey who you are and what you stand for from the outset, your authenticity will come across.

Consider how you can uniquely express the value of being your customer through your welcome. Examples range from personal outreach (e.g., a phone call or hand-written note) to a gift that ties to your company's values and the work you're going to do with your customer. It could be food. It could be a book. It could be fun and frivolous or somber and serious. You can vary your welcome to reflect your company and your customers.

This welcome is about launching a relationship by saying, "We're glad you're here." It's not about transacting business. It's a moment of interpersonal connection.

One client of mine was a bricks-and-mortar apparel retailer whose bullseye aimed to make every customer feel cherished and included. The company decided to use sachets as a welcome gift for new customers for a couple of reasons. First, the ingredients of the potpourri inside the sachet were sweet and spicy, which tied into the brand and their selection of merchandise. Second, since a sachet doesn't have a size, it always fits. This welcome gift was directly connected to the company's inclusivity bullseye. When they found a local artisan to make the sweet and spicy potpourri sachets, the store's owners included their employees' opinions in crafting the idea and building the scent profile. As a result, the employees felt a sense of ownership in the process. The had fun explaining why the sachet represented the store, and their enthusiasm was infectious.

The more you can articulate what makes your company special and build it into your welcome, the more it will resonate for the customers most inclined toward loyalty. It may not resonate deeply with everyone, and that's okay. You're aiming for the hearts of the loyal few.

A good welcome will feel personal and sincere to the recipient. Note that the operative word is feel. Something that feels personal doesn't mean a human being at your company must individually welcome every new customer. While that can be right for some companies, it's not always feasible. Even when it's feasible, it's not always the right decision for a company. If your welcome is automated, it needs to feel special to the person who receives it. If you can't manage the process in-house, there's a whole industry of companies that personalize gifts and handwrite cards. Offerings range from luxe to budget friendly.

The welcome is a great way to share the distinctive personality of your company. Companies that successfully use a customer welcome often choose to embrace the opportunity to have a little fun with the moment. Your welcome has to be appropriate for your company's products and services, but it doesn't have to be boring.

Hit the Target with Your Welcome

One additional benefit for my client who used sachets as a welcome was that employees advised customers to put the gift in their clothing drawers. Every day, when customers opened those drawers, they were greeted with the sweet and spicy scent that reminded them of the store. Engaging multiple senses further embedded the store into its customers' psyche.

An unexpected bonus for the store was that customers loved the thought and gift so much they took pictures of the sachet and put them on social media. Since the sachet was introduced, the store has added new and fun contests and customer appreciation moments to their welcome program, making it a thread that ties customers to the store beyond the initial welcome. As you build your program, consider what might motivate your customers to share your welcome with their social media networks.

Yes, a welcome generally has a cost. Before we worked together, my retail client offered a discount, usually 20 percent off, for new customers. With an average purchase of one hundred dollars, that discount shaved twenty dollars off the top of that first sale. By switching to the sachet, which cost just a few dollars, the store maintained its margin and launched the customer relationship without setting the precedent of a discount.

Even if your welcome is as simple as a phone call to your new customer, you'll apply time to the effort. Some companies immediately see the value and consider a welcome to be a good investment in the long-term customer relationship.

That's not always the case.

My retail client, for example, wasn't initially sold on the idea. They had low margins, and although they were already giving away a discount, they were hesitant to invest in customers who might not come back. Even after they realized the sachets would cost less than the discount, they were skeptical. Fortunately, they were willing to test the power of the welcome at my suggestion.

Customers were thrilled with the thoughtful gift. It changed the tone of their interaction with the company. Customers relied less on discounts to connect with the store and more on an upgraded experience. The value of those little sachets became a huge factor in improving the store's margins. Profitability shot up and so did customer loyalty.

Another client of mine runs B2B training programs. His customers are business owners and members of corporate leadership groups within companies. He wants his customers to feel engaged in the training when they show up. One person's negative energy can impact an entire training group, so there's a direct benefit for my client to set the right tone with his welcome.

To achieve this, he sends a gift box that includes a journal, nice pen, and fun brain teasers that customers are invited to ponder before they arrive for training. The brain teasers aren't part of his functional training, but he ties them into the conversations. He also sends what he calls "thought snacks." Each snack includes an explanation of why he selected it and a silly, invented reason why it will boost participation at the upcoming training. Everything is designed to align aesthetically with his brand in ways that connect to the heart of his company. The gift box is a great expression of his brand and is directly tied to his objective, which is to manage expectations and get people in the right mindset for the training. When customers show up with a positive frame of mind, outcomes are improved. This inspires successful training sessions, which ultimately promotes long-term loyalty.

The design and execution of your welcome is important to its success. Missteps can create problems. Here are a few pitfalls to avoid when you design your welcome program.

Beware of Missing Your Target

If your welcome isn't tied to a unique and thoughtful expression of who you are as a company, it will fail to build the emotional connection your company seeks. No matter how well-intentioned, if your welcome doesn't achieve your goals, you miss the target.

Recently my husband and I purchased new kitchen cabinets. About a week later, a care package from the cabinet manufacturer arrived at our door. Inside the package was a note thanking us for our purchase along with a selection of meats, cheeses, and chocolates. It was unexpected and very nice. After the cabinets were installed, a second care package arrived. This one contained an apron, cookbook, cookbook stand, and mugs with the company logo on them. Again, the gift was unexpected and fancier than I would have imagined. Someone spent a lot of time, consideration, and money on these gifts.

But here's the problem: what was the company's objective for this welcome? As generous as the gifts were, it was not clear how they were supposed to affect my future behavior. Was I expected to keep the branded items until the next time I renovated my kitchen? Was I supposed to love the cookbook enough to refer my friends to the brand? Should I have remembered the long-gone cheese or chocolate? As much as I appreciated the gifts, I couldn't understand the company's strategy.

It probably would have cost less to send a small kitchen cabinet accessory that would have offered long-term value for my new kitchen while also sparking the idea that the company offered even more options to customize my cabinets after the installation. Making that accessory custom-built for the company's cabinets might have inspired me to consider them for future upgrades. Instead, I wondered whether the lavish gifts meant I'd overpaid for my cabinets.

A welcome isn't just a greeting. It's the beginning of a relationship, and, as such, it should be tied to a bigger picture. A welcome should be strategic, not merely a friendly gesture. This cabinet company's lovely gesture missed the mark—at least it did for me. Perhaps they weren't aiming for their bullseye or didn't have a bullseye. Or maybe I didn't understand the gesture because I wasn't destined to be one of their loyal customers.

Consider Compliance

Beyond finding the right welcome, your biggest barrier to results will be internal compliance. Here's where the delicate dance between personalization and consistency comes into play. The more you personalize outreach, the better your chances will be of tapping into an emotional connection. But as you personalize outreach, your good intentions can go awry if it becomes more complicated for your employees to execute the strategy.

I recently purchased some new speakers for my office. Soon after, I opened my mailbox and found a postcard from the company. My initial reaction was positive. Any outreach is better than no outreach. Even better, the postcard was handwritten from the sales team. It said, "Enjoy your purchase of the speakers!" It was signed with the sales rep's first name. In the realm of cultivating loyalty, it was close to an effective welcome, but ultimately, it failed to generate the personal connection necessary to generate any real loyalty.

It's easy to imagine how the idea to send handwritten postcards evolved from inception to reality. I'd be willing to bet the company envisioned their sales team sending genuine notes that would inspire a personal connection. An internal metric might have been tied to compliance. So they got compliance, but only in the barest possible terms. My guess is that the outcome didn't match the intention because the company failed to get its employees on board in a way that translated into cultivating loyalty. Training, reinforcement, and a process to get employees to embrace the program might have ensured a better interaction with customers. I'm guessing that support wasn't provided, and the company lost an opportunity as a result.

Remember, the bar is low because your competitors probably don't do anything to welcome new customers. A postcard is better than nothing, but "enjoy your purchase" is unlikely to make people feel warm and fuzzy at a level that inspires loyalty.

Design Your Welcome Program

When you design your welcome program, use the five factors covered in chapter 2 as a guide. Those five factors are:

- Prioritize emotional connection.
- Create a process with clear goals.
- Break your goals into measurable steps.
- Apply tracking and metrics.
- Add celebration.

As you design your welcome, consider the impact on your team. Your welcome will function best when it's easily added to your team's existing workload. Consider how your team members might try to take shortcuts with your welcome. Then consider how to discourage or compensate for those impulses. The more you understand how your welcome might be undermined, the better you can combat such problems before they arise.

It's more valuable to have a simple welcome that will be executed consistently than to have one that's so big and complicated that it gets buried under its own weight. Small, consistent steps make a big difference in launching a welcome that successfully enhances long-term customer value.

CHAPTER 8

Find High-Impact Moments to Grow the Customer Relationship

Your welcome is only the first moment of engagement with your customers. From there, you extend your customer relationship with an onboarding sequence and ongoing interaction that leads to additional purchases, referrals, and engagement. To create loyalty, these interactions are designed to reinforce customers feeling seen, heard, and valued.

Design Your Onboarding Sequence for Immediate Success

An onboarding sequence is the series of steps that immediately follows your welcome. Onboarding shows customers how to use the products and services they purchased from your organization.

Every company benefits from an onboarding sequence of some kind, whether your company is B2B or B2C. It begins the second your welcome ends and is finished when your customer has the information they need to successfully use your products and services.

As you create your onboarding sequence, consider both the external, customer-facing elements and the internal mechanisms that ensure your team delivers the sequence consistently.

Your onboarding sequence should both give your customers the information they need and also build the customer relationship you want with them.

Give Customers the Information They Need

You want customers to get value from their purchase. Your onboarding sequence should be designed to help them see that value quickly. That means you should understand what your customers need to successfully use your products and services. You don't have to have a complex product or service to have an onboarding sequence. Even if customers purchase something as small as a pen, they deserve to understand why your company is the best place for their future pen needs. That said, someone who buys a pen needs a vastly different onboarding sequence than a customer who has to integrate software into a business setting. Every company has valuable information to share with new customers; however, the more complex the purchase, the more help they will need getting set up.

No matter how simple or complex your sequence might be, onboarding goes through a defined series of steps. These steps can be rolled out to your customers according to a set schedule that you share with them in advance. For example, if your onboarding sequence is a series of ten email messages, tell customers they will receive a series of ten email messages. Sharing a clear map of the onboarding sequence manages expectations as you launch the business relationship, which, in turn, builds trust. When people feel they're on a good path, there's less opportunity for confusion, frustration, or, worse, a change of heart about their decision to purchase.

If you sell complex business solutions, you'll want to build a multifaceted onboarding sequence that might include a combination of automated email messages, online resources, and training, whether virtual, live, or both. Customers might need to be led through a sequence, while also having the freedom to guide themselves to the parts of your solution that matter most to them. The specifics of your onboarding sequence will vary according to the solution you provide. Your thoughtful design will be tailored to your business and your customers' needs.

Build the Relationship You Want

Once you've mapped out the informational elements of your onboarding sequence, add ways to show customer appreciation. This is your opportunity to show customers they are seen, heard, and valued. To do this, go beyond the nuts and bolts of how to use your product or service. Reaffirm the connection with the person who made the purchase and the folks you'll be interacting with, if those are different people. When you add moments of intentional connection into your customer onboarding sequence, it becomes easier to build relationships. It also creates a competitive advantage. Building the relationship is the aspect of onboarding that most businesses, including your competitors, will likely fail to deliver.

Once you've mapped out the informational elements of your onboarding sequence, add ways to show customer appreciation.

Ask yourself:
- How can we include specific moments to reestablish our customer's feeling of being seen, heard, and valued?
- What's the next relationship-building interaction we want customers to experience after our welcome?

These moments of connection should reinforce your core customer message. Your onboarding sequence, like your overall customer relationship, needs heart and smart.

To build long-term relationships, make customer interaction genuine and personal. Share a little bit about who you are as a company and the people behind your products and services. Talk about your values and goals. Show your customers what loyalty looks like in your organization.

Customers don't always know how to be loyal. You can educate them by sharing stories that illustrate how successful clients engaged with your company. These stories should be conversations, not moments to upsell. Stories that demonstrate ways customers have gone beyond operational interaction with your company model the behavior you want customers to practice.

If you want customers to value the benefits of loyalty, show them how it's done. For example, if you want customers to provide testimonials, you should demonstrate how to share testimonials and explain why they're mutually beneficial. Some companies don't explain how customers can act like lucrative loyals, and then they get frustrated when customers don't upgrade their relationship. Be clear and specific to make it easy for customers to choose action.

Some customers will simply "get it." These are the customers who were destined to become loyal. Other customers are busy. They might not intrinsically know the value of loyalty unless you explain it to them. Some customers may start out as limited loyals.

They may become so enamored with what you offer that they ultimately become lucrative loyals. Limited loyals can choose to uplevel their experience with you, but first they first have to appreciate and value loyalty.

Your onboarding sequence ends when you've shared sufficient information for customers to launch successfully as users of your products and services.

Identify Your Inflection Points

Once your customer completes their onboarding sequence, they begin a pattern of ongoing interaction with you that lasts the entire length of their customer relationship. These moments are called inflection points. Every company has its own set of inflection points. You can find your inflection points by understanding your customers' lifecycle with your company. Over time, as customers use your products and services, they'll have needs. When customer needs arise, you'll find inflection points. When you can predict those inflection points and reach out proactively, you improve the customer experience and boost loyalty.

Sometimes inflection points will be about business. Other times, you'll engage to reinforce the customer relationship. Either way, inflection points are predetermined moments to reconnect with customers as you target loyalty.

Find the Inflection Points for Business

To identify inflection points, think about the experience of being your customer from the customer's perspective.

Something as simple as a postcard from your dentist reminding you of a semi-annual cleaning is an inflection point. Dentists know patients are unlikely to remember without prompting, and lost time means lost revenue. Let's face it, without a reminder, it's easy for that twice-a-year checkup to happen every nine months. This might seem insignificant to the patient, but for the dentist, it means three visits every two years instead of four—a 25 percent reduction in revenue. Reminders mean better oral care for patients and more revenue for dentists. To manage the inflection point, dentists must make sure customers get those reminders early enough to easily make biannual appointments.

Consider a software company with one-year customer contracts. The company has discovered that customers who haven't achieved a certain level of product adoption by the third month are less likely to renew at the end of the year. Non-renewal after the first year means the customer was acquired at a loss because the cost of customer acquisition is high.

For this company, one-on-one quarterly business reviews for the first year are inflection points that are delivered as features for customers. Since the onboarding sequence takes two months, the quarterly review means the company has baked in an opportunity to sit down with the customer one month after onboarding ends. This review gives the company a way to learn how the customers are using the product. The review also manages expectations as needed and provides an avenue to troubleshoot customer issues proactively, ensuring that the company gets ahead of any problems from the outset.

To identify your business's inflection points, consider the moments when a customer might need a little more to prompt additional engagement.

In this context, "more" could mean:
- Information.
- Services.
- Reminders.
- Help.

Then, map a timeline of those key moments and create an internal process to engage appropriately in those moments. Notice that triggering inflection points is your responsibility, not your customer's. Cultivating loyalty means meeting your customers where they are rather than hoping they come to you. Putting information on your website or sending a blog post is unlikely to generate the outcomes you want. Customers are busy, so it's your responsibility to reach out when you want them to take action.

Similarly, you have an opportunity to understand your customer's business to engage their loyalty. Sometimes inflection points are triggered by activity in your customer's world. If a B2B customer experiences a hiring surge, firing spree, or acquisition, it's likely to shift usage patterns in ways that can affect the customer's need for your products or services. A B2C customer might move, change jobs, or shift lifestyle habits in ways that affect their need for what you offer. These moments are also inflection points, but they can be harder to capture.

For example, Target famously identified a "pregnancy prediction" by looking at patterns of customers' purchases. The company's predictive models have been honed to the point that they can narrow a woman's due date to a short window, which helps them identify that customer's needs for specific products. This type of technology-driven algorithm is one way to track inflection points for customers.

You might also create a less technology-driven process for checking in with customers according to a set timeline. By making these check-ins consistent, you create inflection points to capture important shifts in customers' needs.

Being specific about your expectations for inflection points helps everyone on your team. You provide prompts and measurable goals for team members to reach out to customers. You give team members a structured way to make sure they follow up about important elements of the customer's experience.

When team members have clear instructions for the information you want them to capture, it's easier for them to be successful. Sometimes the idea of regular connection sounds great, but companies fail to execute according to their good intentions. By making inflection points measurable, you can hold team members accountable. Unless these points are built into employee objectives, it's just too easy for them to get buried under the day-to-day activities of work.

Even a small slowdown in customer outreach can have a big impact on customer relationships and revenue. By creating clear expectations, you also rightsize your expectations for employees. Set expectations on a timeline to stress-test whether your requirements are realistic. Aim for everyone to be successful. If you're asking too much of employees, eventually they'll stop complying with your expectations. Maybe they'll feel frustrated, get burned out, or quit. Either way, that's a loss for your company and your customer.

The Risk of Neglecting Inflection Points

Your system can and likely should employ a combination of tactics to engage with customers across inflection points. Some tactics may be automated, such as sending a tailored email message or helpful resource. Others may be personalized, such as a business review meeting or phone call. The products and services you provide will shape which levers you use for each inflection point. Generally, companies use a combination of mass/automated and personal/tailored outreach. With today's technology, it's easier to use an automated approach to deliver a personalized message. That's a good thing and potential pitfall.

When customers receive a message from you that's addressed to them individually, it can build rapport. But if they receive a message addressed to "Dear [PUT NAME HERE]," you've breached the customer's trust and will have to work harder to regain it. For lucrative loyals who feel seen, heard, and valued by your brand, that breach of trust can damage the connection. Or they may be more forgiving. You can't know in advance how they'll react, so it's better if you never find out. Attention to the details of interaction matters.

Successfully managing inflection points means having a plan for communication and action. Don't wait for customers to start a conversation after onboarding. Waiting can mean you risk losing momentum in the relationship, which leaves a lot of money on the table. This is true for a few reasons.

Successfully managing inflection points means having a plan for communication and action.

If you wait for customers to initiate the connection, you miss opportunities to be top of mind with them. If you have to wait for them to think about your company, you might wait a long time. You might wait forever. When customers aren't thinking about your company, they aren't engaging with your company. Gaps in engagement can negatively impact loyalty. People are busy and are bound to see a lot of competing marketing messages.

If you're not effectively putting your message in front of your customers, it's easy for them to forget you and end up buying from your competitors. It's easy to fall off a customer's radar when the interaction ends. That doesn't mean you should bombard your customers with marketing messages. Annoying them won't promote loyalty either. Like any relationship, too much or too little are both problematic. You're going for the Goldilocks balance of just right. "Just right," in this context, means you know the inflection points and have an action plan to manage your customers' path from one inflection point to the next.

The Risks of Waiting for Customers

Sometimes my clients say, "Our customers love us." Even folks whose businesses are objectively failing have been known to wax rhapsodic about how much their customers love them.

Digging into the reality of what "love" means, it often becomes clear that customers receive a good experience when they actively engage with the business. Once they leave, however, there is little to no interaction. Companies might send email messages. They might announce sales or distribute information about new products, but these communications don't translate into loyalty. They can be part of an engagement process, but they're not the whole process.

If you wait for customers to engage, you'll likely miss problems that surface for customers. In almost every business interaction, there are issues. Some are minor and easily fixed. Others are larger and more cumbersome. When small issues aren't addressed, they fester and become bigger issues. Small issues can get in the way of long-term loyalty. Big issues definitely get in the way. It's important to be proactive in identifying and addressing problems for customers so you can catch small issues quickly.

A company that proactively resolves a problem for a customer, and resolves it well, is more likely to retain that customer. Proactive problem-solving can even enhance loyalty. And proactive problem-solving with sincere empathy makes the biggest difference.

The Carey School of Business found that when companies made a mistake, the way they responded affected customer loyalty. When customers complained, 37 percent were generally satisfied with the interaction when the company offered them something of monetary value, such as a refund or credit. When the company added an apology to the compensation, satisfaction doubled to 74 percent. You can improve loyalty even when an interaction was the result of a business problem.

Your company will never be perfect. Customer mistakes will happen. A plan for well-designed and executed inflection points can catch a slip before it becomes a slide down to customer turnover. If you don't have a plan to engage with your customers, they may become unhappy. Most unhappy customers won't tell you they're unhappy. They'll just leave.

CHAPTER 9

Recognize and Celebrate Your Loyal Customers

C ompanies that do a good job recognizing and celebrating their customers have a huge competitive advantage, which better positions them to develop lucrative loyals. When you recognize and celebrate your customers, you're well positioned to make them feel appreciated. We've talked about celebration in general terms. This chapter takes a closer look at systems for recognition and celebration as tools to show customers how much you value them.

Recognition is initiated by customer action. When a customer does something and your company identifies it and responds, that's recognition. Recognition lets a customer know their action is appreciated, but the action originates with them, not you.

Celebration, on the other hand, is driven by you. Your organization identifies a trigger to initiate an action that makes individual customers feel special. The specific way you make them feel special is the celebration. Celebration lets customers know you appreciate them, and the action originates with you, not them.

Here are a few of the messages you convey when you recognize and celebrate your customers:

- You aren't just one of a gazillion nameless, faceless customers. We see you as an individual.
- You talked about our company, and we heard you.
- You showed your loyalty, and we cherish that. We value your business.
- We appreciate you.
- You matter.

Those are powerful messages.

When you show customers you recognize them and celebrate their engagement with you, you are well positioned to generate true connection.

When you show customers you recognize them and celebrate their engagement with your company, you're well positioned to generate a true connection, and connection generates loyalty. Recognition and celebration are additional ways to demonstrate that your customers are seen, heard, and valued. Recognition and celebration are also great ways to differentiate your company. They are easy and enjoyable ways to set yourself apart from your competitors. Very few companies activate recognition and celebration well on a consistent basis, so harnessing them is an underutilized opportunity to cultivate loyalty.

Almost every business can point to moments when customers were recognized for being valuable.

Here's a story my friend Bob shared with me.

"About fifteen years ago," Bob said, "after my first child was born, we were living in a rental building in Manhattan with a coin-operated laundry in the basement. Our daughter was colicky and vomiting, and we were doing a lot of laundry. I went to my local bank branch, where I was a 'gold' customer, whatever that means, and I asked for two hundred dollars in quarters. The bank refused my request because I wasn't a commercial customer. I called a man at First Republic Bank who had been courting my business and asked him if he could help. He offered to messenger me one hundred dollars in quarters every Monday at no charge. I moved my account to his bank immediately and have done all my personal and professional banking with them ever since then. My business has included half a dozen mortgages and about twenty active professional and personal accounts. I've told this story many times. I refer everyone I can to First Republic."

Is this a great story about the kind of recognition and celebration I'm talking about? It depends.

When it comes to recognition and celebration for customer loyalty, there's a difference between a single employee making a gesture that generates a loyal customer versus a reliable system that cultivates loyalty. If Bob's new banker acted independently, his action was great for his portfolio of clients, but it wouldn't necessarily be a systematic approach for the bank to cultivate loyalty. First Republic would have to formalize their process for customer experiences like Bob's and make them the norm in order for this example to qualify as a true recognition system for long-term loyalty.

Without a system for recognition and celebration, individual people in your company apply ad hoc tactics to customers at random. These tactics might work, or they might not. With ad hoc tactics, you don't have a strategy, consistency, or a way to measure your progress. You might think one action was a homerun when it wasn't. You might completely miss the grand slam.

Systems for recognition and celebration require structure and consistency so team members have a clear understanding of expectations. Consistent processes can be duplicated and repeated across your company. You can evaluate outcomes and assess results. You're in a better position to identify which customers are inclined to become loyal.

The five factors are your guide to applying recognition and celebration that's strategic, consistent, and measurable. While recognition and celebration often go hand in hand, they can exist independently as tools to inspire long-term loyalty.

Recognition Grows Loyalty

Recognition is an ongoing process of making customers feel appreciated when they take some kind of action. Recognition moments become part of your standard operating procedure for customer experience.

For example, suppose a customer makes a second purchase within three months. You know that customers who buy twice within a quarter are more likely to become long-term users of your product or service. You send a thank you card with a personalized note to the customer. Or suppose a customer writes a positive review of your company online. You see the review and write an appreciative response that the customer will be likely to see.

When companies track social media and other customer feedback, they often focus on complaints. Bad word-of-mouth can be expensive. But there's also a cost to ignoring compliments.

When customers feel their compliments are being ignored, they have less incentive to continue spreading positive word-of-mouth. You have the opportunity to show customers who compliment your company the appreciation they deserve. Creating a system to recognize positive customer actions is all upside for your company.

By design, recognition doesn't mean big gestures. It means small gestures that build trust over time.

Brené Brown is a researcher whose work focuses on vulnerability and shame, which are big inhibitors to growth and leadership. She compares building trust to a marble jar. Every time someone takes an action to build trust, it's like putting a marble in a jar. When someone does something that undermines trust, it's like taking a marble out. You don't start a relationship by sharing your deepest secrets and vulnerabilities. That's a level of trust that grows over time. You build up to that point marble by marble. When the jar is full of marbles, trust has been earned. The kinds of actions that are worthy of marbles aren't big. In fact, they're just the opposite. They're the small actions of being seen, heard, and valued.

The same principle applies to recognition. Each point of recognition may represent a small marble, but over time, the marbles add up. A full marble jar means a higher likelihood of customer loyalty.

Recognition isn't a time to sell. When companies conflate recognition and selling, it undermines the recognition. All of a sudden, recognition feels like a cheesy or even smarmy money grab. Companies lose integrity when recognition comes with a sales pitch.

Paying attention to purchase patterns and knowing when customers are talking about your company online are just two places where you can insert recognition. Recognition requires a thoughtful, consistent process that identifies and interacts with customers' actions throughout their relationship with your company.

Add Celebration to Further Boost Loyalty

Some customer actions deserve more than simple recognition. When recognition isn't a sufficient expression of your appreciation, it's time to unleash celebration.

Celebration is triggered when companies identify something about their customers that they want to glorify. There are two kinds of celebration: ongoing celebration and random acts of celebration.

Ongoing celebration is a way of recognizing customers as the people behind their purchases. It shows you value them as more than their financial contribution.

Celebrating a customer's birthday is a simplistic example of celebration. Celebrating birthdays shows you know customers well enough and care about them sufficiently to acknowledge something that's purely about them. It shows that something about them matters to you.

While a birthday celebration is about your customer, it doesn't build the relationship. Many consumers think it's odd for commercial enterprises to send them birthday cards. They see "get a free dessert" on your birthday as being promotional code for, "By the way, pay for a meal while you're here and bring all your friends to buy meals, too."

Not to mention, other companies also engage with customers on their birthdays, so there's competition for your customer's attention. Why lump your company in with the rest? There are better ways of celebrating your customers.

For example, when a customer makes a referral to you, it's a big deal. Your customer put their reputation on the line for you and gave you a huge gift, a new customer. Validate that customer's generosity with celebration. I worked with an executive coach who sent a gift worth more than a thousand dollars to any client who referred a new customer to him after that new customer had worked with him for ninety days. He didn't talk about it because he wanted to make sure the referrals were genuine. He knew his new customers would stick around a while once they hit the ninety-day mark.

Very few companies do celebration well, so it's another opportunity to differentiate your customer experience from competitors. Crafting a celebration program is also fun. You get to show your company's personality in ways that your lucrative loyals will particularly relish. Celebration is a place where you get to think creatively about your lucrative loyals. By knowing them and celebrating them, you can inspire them to be even more dedicated to your company.

Celebrations are more complex than recognitions. Recognitions are consistent, quick hits. Celebrations carry more weight. That's why it's important to be clear about the outcome you want to achieve with those customers who are most inclined toward loyalty.

Because celebrations are aimed at specific and special interactions, companies often choose to tailor their celebration plans by customer segment. Your lucrative loyals will receive a different level of celebration than your average customers. Maybe you want to develop a celebration campaign as an attempt to convert lazy or limited loyals. Or not. Your unique business will dictate the amount of time, effort, and money you apply to your celebration strategy.

Like many elements of cultivating loyalty, your celebration strategy can evolve over time. Start with a small, simple way to celebrate customers that you can activate consistently. Develop internal mechanisms to weave the celebration into the everyday fabric of your company. Enjoy the outcomes.

Celebrations don't have to cost a lot of money. In fact, they can be free. One of my clients has successfully used a personal phone call from the CEO to the company's most loyal customers to celebrate the anniversary of their first purchase. This strategy wouldn't work for every company or every CEO. But for this company's loyal customers, it's a great act of celebration. Celebration efforts succeed when activating your bullseye triggers positive feelings that inspire loyalty.

Add Random Acts of Celebration

Sometimes it's worth going all out to make a customer feel special. There's a form of celebration that's worth unleashing in those special cases: the random act of celebration. This strategy is designed to make a statement. It's not something you can or will want to do a lot. Its randomness is part of its power.

Peter Shankman is the founder of Help a Reporter Out and author of Zombie Loyalists. In addition to focusing on loyalty professionally, it's his nature to be a vocal and loyal customer. One of the companies he loves is Morton's Steakhouse.

One night after doing some serious road warrioring, Shankman boarded a plane home. Realizing he was hungry and would arrive late in the evening, he sent a tweet to Morton's, jokingly asking them to meet him at the airport with a porterhouse steak. When he got off the plane, he was surprised to be approached by a man in a tuxedo who was carrying a bag from Morton's. Inside the bag, Shankman found a twenty-four ounce porterhouse, plus shrimp, potatoes, bread, and cutlery, all gratis. That's an amazing gesture, even for a loyal customer, and, of course, Shankman tweeted about it. A tweet from him is not just any tweet. He has more than 175,000 Twitter followers, so Morton's got fantastic exposure from their act of generosity.

Not only did Shankman's loyalty to Morton's grow exponentially, but he also became even more vocal in his support of the brand. He still tells the Morton's story when he speaks. The story has been written up in articles and books, including this one. And the moment happened in 2011. Was that free dinner worth the cost and effort to Morton's? You bet.

The occasional random act of celebration can deliver exponential returns. Your results will be tied to finding the right customer and making the right offer. In that respect, the "random" act of celebration may seem random for your customer, but it isn't haphazard. From your company's perspective, it's strategic. Who you offer it to, what you offer, and how you expect that customer to respond and engage are all part of your strategy.

And while you can be strategic with your random acts of celebration, they must also be authentic. In this case, Morton's made an authentic and genuine delivery to a loyal customer. It also happened to be smart marketing on their part.

That's the power of a successful random act of celebration.

There's also another lesson in Shankman's story, and that's the power of the ripple effect. When you throw a stone in a pond, the first kerplunk creates a series of ripples that move outward from the spot where the rock hit the water. Those ripples get bigger as they move farther away from the point of engagement. The same holds true for your customer interactions. Every customer connection has the potential to create ripples. Whether it's through word-of-mouth or social media, your loyal customers will talk about their experiences with you. When you do something amazing, they'll tell other people over and over again. In the case of Morton's random act of celebration, the ripple effects encompass every person who has heard about that steak dinner, which now includes you. The story is free advertising for Morton's and also for Shankman, who has dined out on it, literally and figuratively, for years.

Let's Talk about Rewards Programs

Rewards programs compensate customers for taking specific actions. Examples include buy ten and get one free punch cards, referral deals, and discounts for newsletter signups. These programs are often called loyalty programs, but that's not an accurate name. Reward programs are tactics. Cultivating loyalty is a strategy.

Rewards programs can be valuable components of marketing strategies. They have been shown to be effective for short-term motivation. That's why so many companies offer them. Still, a customer who uses your rewards program isn't necessarily a loyal customer. That's because when rewards programs generate some kind of loyalty, it tends to be lazy or limited. Rewards programs rarely inspire lucrative loyalty on their own. Having lazy or limited loyals is beneficial, but those customers don't generate the same levels of long-term profitability as lucrative loyals.

Reward programs are tactics.
Cultivating loyalty is a strategy.

Most rewards programs function best as tools to boost short-term purchases. These programs can be good additions to a marketing plan, but they fall short in vaulting customers into becoming lucrative loyals.

Lucrative loyalty requires a stronger connection between the customer and company. With this in mind, companies can evaluate the results of their rewards programs to determine the short-term and long-term benefits.

No matter which collection of recognition, celebration, and rewards you implement, your goal should be to cultivate loyalty with experiences that inspire customers to feel seen, heard, and valued.

CHAPTER 10

Use Segmentation to Boost Customer Loyalty

From average customers to lazy, limited, and lucrative groups, customers aren't created equal. When you orient your company for loyalty, your customers' experience shouldn't be equal either.

When you divide your customer base into smaller groups, or segments, you're better-positioned to deliver a solution that's tailored for each key segment's needs. Customer segmentation improves loyalty by inviting customers, and particularly lucrative loyals, into an experience that customizes your messages, offerings, interactions, and more to their wants and needs.

Upfront Ventures partner Kara Nortman says, "The biggest mistake people make is treating their customers as averages. Companies say, 'This is our average engagement.' 'This is the average number of times a consumer comes in a month.' Averages are misleading. When you're trying to understand your customers, you need to segment them so you know who uses your product a lot, who hasn't used it at all, and who's starting to use it more. Getting into the detailed patterns of segmented usage is important for learning about your customers."

You can segment your customers based on a variety of parameters. You can segment by revenue and provide a different experience based on the amounts customers spend. You can segment based on demographics, such as gender. A B2C company like Nordstrom might segment customers by zip code, so when January rolls around, they're featuring swimsuits in Miami and sweaters in Michigan. B2B companies might sort customers by industry. Salesforce might talk about its new features one way with consultants and a different way with manufacturers.

Not all customer segmentation strategies work effectively to improve loyalty. Sometimes companies create segments that generate complexity with little real value. Data is useful to understand and define customer segments, but it's easy for segmentation strategies to get bloated. Too much data can lead to analysis paralysis. Complex strategies are harder to implement consistently. Too often, companies buckle under the weight of complicated segmentation schemes and then ditch them completely.

This is especially true when companies create customer segments without clear goals. It's hard to hit the target if you don't know where you're aiming. Focusing on your loyalty goals will streamline your segmentation strategy and achieve better results.

Not all customer segmentation strategies work effectively to improve loyalty.

Focus on tailored approaches only for the segments that will generate sufficient gain to justify your effort. Just because you *can* identify a segment doesn't mean you *should* create a specific effort to lure those customers. Lazy loyals, for example, are unlikely to be worth the effort.

Focus on lucrative loyals first. Once you've had initial success, then add more segments. As you identify new customer segments and identify your goals for each segment, implement customer experiences that are adapted to each segment.

By starting with lucrative loyals, you already have a group of customers you've identified as being worthy of segmentation. Creating an elevated customer experience for lucrative loyals is a great place to start.

Other companies can choose to take segmentation further. Your lucrative loyals are probably not a homogeneous group. Reexamine your lucrative loyals to identify further segmentation within that group of customers. If you find even more ways to customize interaction with lucrative loyals, you can refine your marketing to enhance their experiences with your company for even better results.

Use Customer Segmentation for Marketing

Refining your definition of a lucrative loyal by applying additional segmentation allows you to target smaller groups based on specific characteristics within your pool of lucrative loyals. My manufacturing client whose bullseye was "less is more" sold products to medical professionals and retail outlets. While those industries are very different, the company successfully served lucrative loyals in both markets. The company realized that the selling points for their medical loyals weren't the same as the selling points for their retail loyals.

The company created separate marketing campaigns for each industry segment and tailored its messages for those campaigns to the needs of each group. The marketing materials gave the impression that the company sold completely different products to the two groups. In fact, the products were identical. The features and benefits that loyal customers in the medical field valued weren't the same as the features and benefits that the loyal retailer customers prioritized.

Sometimes the two segments mingled. Retailers saw the company's products at a doctor's office. Doctors shopped in retail environments. In each environment, customers saw the differentiated marketing messages. That was okay because my client prepared for this eventuality.

Ensure Consistency between Segments

You can create different messages for separate segments of lucrative loyals. But—and this is a big but—*only* if you apply a non-negotiable rule to ensure that segmentation enhances loyalty: your marketing messages to each group can't be contradictory; they must be consistent to maintain and build trust with your key segments.

Sometimes a customer can belong to two segments. They might receive two different sets of advertising messages. If that happens, those messages must be consistent. The most important rule of segmentation marketing is to be consistent in all of your segmented marketing messages. Consistent doesn't mean identical; rather, it means customers shouldn't receive conflicting messages.

A prospect who hears conflicting messages may be confused, at best, or, worst case, may decide not to buy from your company at all. A lucrative loyal who hears a conflicting message may lose confidence in their relationship with your company.

Let's go back to the example of my manufacturing client who sells in both medical and retail markets. Customers receive marketing messages that were crafted for distinct sets of lucrative loyals, whether medical or retail. Those messages may be different, but they're not contradictory. Retail customers might learn about different attributes of the products they already buy, but they shouldn't encounter any marketing messages that undermine the information they've received from the medical sector. If marketing messages are contradictory, they create confusion. Confusion degrades customers' trust, even on a subconscious level. Loss of trust is a devastating blow to loyalty.

To help ensure consistency, assume that every potential customer will see every marketing message. The heart of your brand must come through as a singular foundation of your company. Specific messages will vary from segment to segment. That's what segmentation is all about. Those messages just shouldn't contradict each other.

Today's world of online marketing makes targeting customer segments easier, but not every customer group fits neatly into social media searches. You can slice and dice data by zip code, but not all customers are so easy to categorize.

Craig Wedren is a film and TV composer for such shows as School of Rock, Wet Hot American Summer, and Glow. In the 1990s, he was the lead singer for a band called Shudder to Think. Shudder to Think had a cult-like following of loyal fans. When the band broke up in 1998, there was no social media to stay connected with fans. Today, Wedren balances his composing work with solo music and wants to reconnect with Shudder to Think's fans.

He says, "My team and I are figuring out which rocks to turn over to connect or reconnect with fans and potential fans. Once people are on board, they're loyal. It's just hard to know where they are, how to find them, and how to reconnect with them. That's especially true of adults over forty who used to be fans of Shudder to Think. The challenge for me and the fun of it is getting underneath the hood of these [social media] platforms to try to see how their algorithms work." By engaging fans, Wedren builds his audience. He's an artist, but his art is his business as well.

Once Wedren identifies key characteristics of his fans, he can tailor messages to speak to segments of fans with shared attributes. Speaking to the heart of your customers with messages designed expressly for them is the best way to affirm your customers' decision to be loyal.

Segmentation for Customer Experience

Beyond marketing messages, segmentation that differentiates customer experience is a key to developing lucrative loyals. If customers aren't all equal, they shouldn't receive equal experiences.

The notion that products, services, upgrades, and other aspects of the customer experience should benefit lucrative loyals can be controversial. All customers deserve a positive, respectful experience. Their purchase has earned them no less. But a customer who begins a relationship with your company at an average level may be inspired to upgrade into greater loyalty. A well-designed segmentation strategy provides an experience that invites customers to want more. As customers deepen their relationship with you, segmentation means they get access to benefits reserved for customers who earned elevated status.

Experiential segmentation can include just about any advantage. Consider offering these perks:

- To make sure your best customers save time, give them preferential access to your team with direct access to dedicated support and additional avenues for upgraded customer service.

- Offer your high-value segments ways to sign up early for your events, conferences, and other limited-access perks. Then give them VIP access and experiences.
- Ensure that high customer lifetime value segments get personal outreach. Use automated engagement for segments with lower customer lifetime value for your company.

Consider how you can create an upgraded experience for your most lucrative and loyal customer segments at every point in the customer lifecycle. Use your inflection points to add moments of connection and celebration that set a loyal customer's experience apart from the rest.

The Downside of Free Stuff

Gifts and other freebies require special consideration. Branded merchandise or other free stuff isn't a magic rocket ship to an upgraded experience. Gifts can be part of the answer (hey, we all like gifts!), but if long-term loyalty is your goal, freebies aren't the entire solution. Gifts that aren't tied to a comprehensive strategy that makes your customers feel seen, heard, and valued will be wasted. Freebies and gifts work best when they're part of a bigger plan that's designed to keep your segmented lucrative loyals' preferences in mind.

Segmentation Is a Moving Target

Segmentation strategies would be easier if customers acted the same way all the time. Unfortunately, they don't. Instead, customers' usage patterns shift. An average customer might love what you offer so much they opt into becoming a lucrative loyal. Conversely, a loyal customer may downgrade their relationship with you. Segmentation for loyalty relies on your ability to assign and reassign customer segments based on customers' changing use of your products and services.

Successful segmentation means you have well-defined ways to continually identify lucrative loyals and assign them to a segment. Create clear guidelines for your team so they can easily manage customer experiences for each of your defined segments.

Segmentation for loyalty relies on your ability to assign and reassign customer segments based on customers' changing use of your products and services.

Segmentation for customer experience begins with the welcome. While you have an opportunity to thoughtfully welcome every customer in a way that sets your company apart from your competitors, consider that first purchase. Are there aspects of a customer's first interaction that might identify their potential as a lucrative loyal?

As the customer's experience continues through the inflection points, identify additional markers of engagement that classify a customer's segment based on their inclination toward loyalty:

- How will you make the segmentation decision?
- What does a change in segment mean for the customer?
- Is that message conveyed to the customer? Or does it happen behind the scenes?

- Who is responsible for making sure segmentation upgrades are applied to your internal systems for prompting customer-facing action and tracking results?

Managing a segmentation strategy for lucrative loyalty means you know where you're aiming, understand your loyals, have a plan to implement loyalty for your segments, and can reassess segment assignments as circumstances shift.

The better you know your customers, the better you'll be able to identify lucrative loyals. The more targeted your offerings are, the more you'll speak to the heart of those customers who feel increasingly seen, heard, and valued. These virtuous cycles of experience work most effectively when you aim for the segments of your most lucrative loyal customers.

PART IV

Prepare Your Team for Lucrative Loyalty

Internal coordination and engaged employees enable you to drive customer loyalty. This coordination and engagement will require practices that reinforce your company's objectives.

- Design a company culture for employee engagement with customer loyalty.
- Refine the five factors to implement loyalty inside your company.
- Track and measure the right customer data.
- Use feedback effectively.

CHAPTER 11

Engage Your Team

I t can be helpful to think of your team as your internal customers. Encourage team members to embrace your customer-facing initiative by creating a culture in which your team also feels seen, heard, and valued.

How employees feel about their work directly impacts how they interact with customers. The key to employee engagement in customer loyalty begins with your internal company culture. When your company's culture is designed for connection, the benefits transfer to your customers.

Upfront Ventures' Mark Suster says, "Culture is everything. People join an organization, and to them, it's much more than a job. People who join your company want to feel like they're joining a mission that's aligned with them. Great leaders, first and foremost, set vision. They tell you what you're trying to achieve, and it can't be BS. It has to be specific and detail-oriented so everyone knows, 'This is what we're trying to achieve.'

"Great leaders then publish objectives to fulfill their vision. They create structure so people know their clear roles and responsibilities. Leaders hold people accountable, positive and negative. And it's measurable.

"People tend to be happier when they know how their contribution leads to the company winning. If you come to work every day and you don't know if you're winning or how you contribute, you're just doing a job."

Most people want more than just a job. They want to be engaged. There are numerous advantages to having engaged employees. In addition to greater job satisfaction, engaged employees have lower absenteeism and higher levels of retention, and they're more likely to be loyal employees. Engaged employees are 17 percent more productive than their less-engaged peers.

Even in industries, such as retail, that are known to churn through employees, companies can create a culture that inspires employees to stick around and be dedicated enthusiasts for their employer. People want to feel that their work matters. This ties back to customer loyalty. Companies that aspire to improve their customer experience to encourage loyalty are more likely to succeed when team members are brought into and have bought into the company's goals. Fusing your culture to your loyalty objectives improves your odds of success.

Customer Experience Needs a Leader

While customer loyalty is part of everybody's job, the responsibility for ensuring a consistent customer experience that builds loyalty must ultimately be assigned to a single person. It's like the old fable of Somebody, Everybody, Anybody, and Nobody: "There was a job to be done, and Anybody could do it. Everybody thought that Somebody would do it, so Nobody did it."

When it comes to customer experience, the process often ends up being nobody's job, and that's a problem.

Customer loyalty needs a designated leader who is specifically tasked to guide the process. That leader has to be able to influence company direction, authorize training, influence changes cross-functionally, and ensure consistency for a unified approach the team can rally behind.

Even if your company isn't big enough to support a designated chief customer officer in the C-suite, assign the responsibility for customer experience to one person who can be effective working across the company. In larger companies, senior executives must champion the cause, but they generally aren't the initiative's day-to-day leaders. Once you identify the person who will lead your customer experience initiative, make it clear to everybody else in your company that the person you chose has the authority to implement the changes. To promote adoption, your entire team needs to believe the person in charge of customer loyalty has the full support of leadership.

In smaller companies, the job may fall to the CEO. When the CEO is in charge, the impediment to adoption tends to be focus. There needs to be a consistent process for everyone to follow, and the CEO has to make time to do the work that ensures customer loyalty becomes reality.

No leader intends to roll out a flavor-of-the-month initiative, yet it happens all the time. There's a big meeting, a speaker, a team-building outing, and some other mechanism for sharing the big new idea. Banners sprout up all over the office.

A short time later, the big idea is nothing but a memory.

Nothing came of it.

Leaders understandably become frustrated when their teams don't engage with an initiative. That frustration can roll downhill to the employees who are, in turn, understandably frustrated when they're asked to engage with an idea but don't have sufficient support to make it successful. Everyone feels the pain.

It doesn't have to be this way.

For customer loyalty to avoid the dreaded flavor-of-the-month predicament, your initiative needs to become your company's new reality. To be successful, you need to embed customer experience into your company culture.

Culture Is for Everybody

The work of company loyalty extends beyond your employees.

Suppose your company hires a social media vendor. The vendor tweets something lunkheaded, and that one foolish tweet gets attention, goes viral, and brings negative attention to the company. Do customers care that the tweet came from a vendor? Not at all. As far as they're concerned, the company owns the responsibility for that tweet. Every team member, including vendors and partners, must be part of the conversation about your loyalty objectives so there's one consistent message to customers.

Company leaders who act in alignment with their own policies shape a culture for consistent customer engagement. When a CEO tells his team to behave one way, then acts like he's above his own policies, it undermines the culture.

The CEO of one small technology startup was adamant that authenticity and transparency were the company's core cultural values. He preached those values to his employees. Then, at a sales meeting, a potential client asked the CEO how many customers the company served. The CEO quoted a number that was more than double the true figure and then asked one of his employees to validate his claim. In that moment, his stated culture of authenticity and transparency was blown.

To build a successful culture, nobody can be exempt from the guidelines your company creates. A culture built for lucrative loyals needs a set of policies that are implemented consistently throughout the organization. No exceptions.

What Culture Isn't

Companies have been known to make well-intentioned but misguided attempts in their quest for a better company culture.

Some companies use snacks, a beer keg, or a foosball table to encourage employees. They think these goodies will support initiatives like customer loyalty. Companies have been known to call that culture, but it's not. These efforts alone fail to create culture because culture doesn't grow from goodies. Culture is much deeper.

Goodies can be components of a great company culture, but they need to be tied to purpose. Goodies without significance are like food without nutrition: empty. And, let's face it. They may taste sweet at first, but like junk food, meaningless gestures leave people feeling unsatisfied. Companies that try to buy culture with beer and foosball find their relationship initiatives wither and die.

How you deliver this message will affect employees' adoption of it. Here's a real-world story that shows what can happen when a company poorly executes good culture-building ideas. A company with employees throughout the United States brought all of them to its headquarters for an all-hands meeting over several days. The executive team planned to kick off the year's growth initiatives and use the time for team building. Since so many employees lived and worked far from the headquarters, one of the stated goals was to help everyone rededicate themselves to the company's mission.

One team leader planned a fun outing for his department. The outing was scheduled to begin at four o'clock, after the day's official meetings ended. After the activity was announced to the team, the company's COO nixed it. The COO's rationale was that employees were being paid for a full week of work and leaving at four wasn't acceptable. The leader who had planned the outing was told there could be "fun after forty," meaning fun would be allowed only after the employees completed forty hours of work.

Cancelling the outing had two outcomes. The team leader was humiliated by being disempowered in front of his team. He believed he had acted in accordance with the company's values and the objective of the meetings. He felt demotivated and soon polished his resume.

The employees didn't respond well either. Many had traveled over the weekend or at night to get to the meeting. They learned that their personal time was negotiable, but the hours from nine to five were sacred.

The incident came from the top of the organization—the office of the COO. And it wasn't the first time something like that had happened. It was more than just a single moment of poor messaging or micromanagement; it embodied the culture of the company.

As a result, employees were less willing to be flexible on the company's behalf since the company had been so inflexible for them. This lesson translated to their customer interactions. These employees were less enthusiastic about making an extra effort for the company and its customers. In the following year, the team leader, several key employees from his department, and numerous valuable customers left the company.

The Cost of Poor Culture

When team members don't feel validated, they take calls from recruiters. And when they get an opportunity to take another job, they leave. Employee turnover is expensive for your organization in many ways:

- Once an employee has quit, it takes time and energy to find, hire, onboard, and train a replacement.
- New employees have a learning curve while they get acclimated to the company's formal procedures.
- A new employee also has to learn the organization's informal norms, which can initially slow down workflow.
- Turnover among employees shifts the team's interpersonal dynamics. Settling in takes time.
- When employees leave, they take institutional knowledge with them, and that knowledge can't be regained.
- Customers have to get used to new contacts, which creates disruption and a period of adjustment.

Turnover also hurts customer loyalty by interrupting communication, eroding trust, and putting stress on the customer relationship. All of these disruptions are expensive and avoidable costs to your company.

Nothing compares to relationships built between people. An engaged, stable team may not guarantee customer success, but a disengaged team with a revolving set of employees will impede your goals for company culture and customer loyalty.

CASE STUDY: URBANSTEMS

UrbanStems is an online flower delivery company that focuses on creating a better gifting experience. Co-founders Ajay Kori and Jeff Sheely believe in creating the best experience for customers. Kori says, "We follow the central hypothesis that if you create the best experience for your customers, you'll always win at the end of the day."

He adds, "We borrowed from Zappos and Mark Lore [who founded Diapers.com and Jet.com before becoming chief executive officer of Walmart e-commerce for the US market]. They believe the first step in creating customer loyalty is having the best experience for your employees. If you're creating a place where people are happy, they're going to create the best experience for your customers. That's an advantage that can't be replicated by a company with unhappy employees."

Kori and Sheely's process for creating happiness begins during the company's first conversation with a prospective employee.

Sheely says, "From interview one, we talk about creating an environment where people are happy. If that idea resonates with the people we're talking with, we continue. If it doesn't, we end the conversation pretty quickly. That way, the emphasis on creating happiness is something new employees care about automatically when they start."

At the outset of any interviewing process, the first hurdle is for the company to feel confident that the prospective employees are brought into the company's philosophy.

Kori says, "The big floral companies have some of the worst customer service on the planet. They're way up there with cable companies and event ticketing companies. People just do not like that floral companies add fees, they're slow, they're unresponsive, they're late, and the flowers don't show up when they're supposed to. And then the flowers die really quickly. Getting flowers delivered can be a terrible experience, and the industry is well-known for that."

Sheely says, "We wanted to do better. In the earliest days of the company, we realized that we were sending flowers, but we were also sending a feeling. What people are really doing when they send flowers is that they're sending, 'I thought of you; I want to send you something.' They're expressing emotion. They're sending happiness. Because that was our philosophy, we designed every step of the experience around that."

You're sending flowers, sure, but what you're really sending is a feeling.

"No matter the reason for sending the flowers, they will brighten the recipient's day and let them know someone cares about them. That experience should make the sender feel happy, too," says Sheely.

UrbanStems designs the receiver's and sender's experience to include a personal touch that's focused on making someone's day better.

Sheely says, "When you're working with flowers, a lot can go wrong. It's a perishable product, and we're trying to deliver it to someone who doesn't know it's coming. It's never going to be 100 percent perfect. When it's less than 100 percent perfect, people call into our customer happiness team. Sometimes people get angry because they think that's the way to get better service. They'll come in guns blazing.

"As soon as they talk to our customer happiness team, they realize somebody cares enough to make it right and help them figure out the problem. Our team comes up with a solution. We understand those flowers are important for the person who receives them. Our team takes care of them and is dedicated to making sure customers are truly happy. That way of interacting changes the mood all around. Listening to some of our customer calls and seeing how quickly people turn around when they realize the person on the line actually cares is amazing.

"To get that outcome, you have to have the right people in the job. It's not an easy job. So, it's about having the right people, but then also empowering them to be solution-oriented. When they come up with ways to fix things, it spreads our mission of happiness.

"We talk about the mission constantly. We're always making sure the team knows that's what we're about. And then we empower them to do whatever it takes to make the mission real. That's true on the customer care side, it's true on the courier side, and it's even true on our corporate team. From the people who are sharing our marketing messaging to the people interacting with our customers, our people are in an environment where we live and breathe everyday happiness."

CHAPTER 12

Apply the Five Factors for Long-Term Success

C ulture confounds a lot of companies, but there's a simple way to develop a strong company culture. Just like customer loyalty, company culture is realized through predictable and positive engagement for employees.

In many ways, culture is a habit.

Habits are created when you do the same thing repeatedly and consistently. Invoicing customers on the first day of the month can be habit. Turning in your TPS reports by four o'clock every Friday can be a habit. And you can create habits that form your company's culture.

> *You can create habits that form your company's culture.*

To inspire your team to embrace customer loyalty, design habits to support a culture where team members, like customers, feel seen, heard, and valued.

The Five Factors to Implement Loyalty

Apply the five factors to your customer loyalty plan so your team understands what's expected of them. This approach to implementation develops team connection to your customer initiative while improving clarity and consistency for action. It prevents flavor-of-the-month syndrome and successfully integrates your customer loyalty initiative into your company. The five factors aren't complex, but they are vital to success.

The five factors are your guide to building culture as a habit:

- Prioritize connection in your company culture.
- Create clear goals to activate your culture.
- Break down the goals into measurable steps and reinforce them consistently.
- Apply tracking and metrics to ensure compliance, course correction, and agile improvement.
- Celebrate culture wins.

Prioritize Your Connection Message for Culture

Team members need a clear vision for the company's objectives so they can see your vision for the customer experience. It's easier for people to rally around an initiative when they're brought into the vision. It's nice to think that team members will share your enthusiasm, but they need a reason to believe in it. As your team recognizes why customer loyalty is important, it becomes easier for them to buy into the concept.

For most companies, the foundation for culture will be aligned with your bullseye message for customers. Your internal message might not be the same as your customer-oriented bullseye message, but it's likely the two messages will share a philosophical foundation.

At ClusterTruck, Chris Baggott made "don't ship maybes" the company's bullseye message. While this message started in the company's kitchens as a guideline for food orders, it grew to represent decision-making throughout the organization. This growth took repetition and coaching so that people throughout the company would understand what "a maybe" was. That bullseye provided a guideline for employees to engage with customers.

Create Clear Goals for Your Culture

As you implement your initiative, create clear goals to help your employees understand the company's direction for customer loyalty. Sharing how the vision ties to your goals provides perspective and supports your team in feeling seen, heard, and valued. Employees are more inclined to become invested in your loyalty initiative when they understand the company's focus and their role in it.

Employees need goals that are clear enough that every employee understands what's expected in order to be successful. It helps when the goals exist as a formal written document that employees can review.

It's also helpful for employees to hear about the goals in a variety of settings. Leaders can share their expectations in multiple ways, using a variety of tactics. Guidelines can be rolled out at an all-hands, in-person meeting like a town hall and then reinforced in videos from the CEO, company newsletters, email messages, and informal communication. A multi-faceted approach to sharing goals throughout the company has a greater likelihood of taking root.

As you articulate your goals, there are some common pitfalls you should avoid. Beware of unspoken expectations. People will pay attention to what you prioritize. If you create a goal that focuses on a higher purpose, but you talk only about generating revenue, your team will know you actually value money over purpose.

If your compensation structure is aligned to support revenue generation—not the higher purpose—employees will still see your true motivator as being money, no matter what you say. Employees are motivated to buy into goals when they see that your actions are consistent with your words.

Employees are self-interested, and they will find ways to make your goal work to their advantage. Wells Fargo learned this lesson the hard way by setting goals for its bank employees to open more accounts. Incentives were applied when more accounts were opened. Naturally, the number of new accounts went up. Unfortunately, the incentives were so appealing that employees opened new accounts for customers who didn't want them. Employees also created fake customers and opened accounts for them, too. Misaligned goals and incentives created huge issues for the bank and massive negative consequences for its brand.

As you set goals, consider how team members might manipulate them for their individual advantage. Any system that offers financial compensation will motivate employees to enhance their self-interest within that system. When employees buy into your company's vision and feel appreciated for their contribution, they're more likely to engage with your goals. Goals will be achieved more readily when your reward system is aligned with a culture where employees feel seen, heard, and valued.

Inc. magazine asked executives at six hundred companies to estimate what percentage of their team could name the company's top three priorities. Executives predicted that 64 percent would be able to name them.

Inc. then asked the company's employees to name the company's top three priorities.

Only 2 percent could do so.

If executives don't ingrain their priorities in the organization, they won't inspire action.

Companies need a plan to share priorities consistently. Plans begin with a message from the top brass, and this message must be reinforced. As the Inc. magazine example suggests, sharing goals isn't a matter of "set it and forget it."

Another way to promote consistency and reinforce your goals is to share them with prospective employees before they're hired, beginning with their first interview. In addition to sharing your goals, interviewers can ask job candidates questions to learn how they demonstrated their commitment to a company's cultural values in previous jobs.

Clearly articulating your expectations for culture has two main benefits. First, your clarity will make it easier to attract candidates who gravitate to your message. It shows job prospects that they will be working for a company with a point of view about customers and culture. Second, sharing your goals frames expectations upfront. When your goals are overtly part of your communication at every stage of the interviewing process, employees show up to their jobs on their first day of work pre-loaded with your important loyalty orientation.

Communication about your goals extends into employee onboarding. Drive home the point that you have a gold standard for customer loyalty with reinforcement for new employees.

You may find it helpful to include goals and specific customer loyalty-related tasks into an employee's initial work plan. Some companies structure employee onboarding with a 30/60/90 plan, which lays out specific hurdles for a new employee to hit in the first thirty, sixty, and ninety days of employment. When you include elements that reinforce your culture of customer loyalty in an employee's 30/60/90 plan, it ensures that these topics will be discussed and implemented.

A culture that's designed for customer loyalty doesn't stop with a new employee's onboarding. Once onboarding is complete, employees will still receive ongoing reinforcement over their term of employment. Team members will see your goals fortified through words and actions in team meetings, annual performance reviews, company outings, and more.

Goals that tie culture to your customer loyalty initiatives probably make perfect sense to company leaders. Team members need more time to ingest those goals. They'll need to hear the goals many times before they sink in. That's because employees are generally focused on their roles, not the company's larger strategic vision.

The role of repetition to ingrain habit has been borne out in research, which shows that repetition has to be deliberate with a clear structure for the habit you're trying to create, and it has to be triggered regularly. This structured approach to repetition creates the neural pathways that ingrain a new habit. If you want your team to be invested in your goals, define each team member's role in achieving those goals.

Break Your Goals into Measurable Steps

In addition to repeating your company's goals for customer experience, give team members a series of action steps to take in support of those goals. After all, your goals for customer loyalty won't materialize overnight. Instead, they will be realized through a series of small, measurable steps. I call these "two-degree shifts."

A two-degree shift is almost imperceptible, so it's easy to make. Yet over time, if you repeatedly alter your course by two degrees, you'll end up in a different place.

Reinforcing goals with two-degree shifts creates an agile process that makes those goals achievable. It's easier to create long-term change when team members get a win and then build from that success. Small shifts also give customers time to acclimate to change. The final advantage of two-degree shifts is that they provide leaders incremental opportunity to evaluate what's working and what isn't.

Achieving change through two-degree shifts isn't as glamorous as a big pivot; however, a series of actionable steps lets a process take root. The shortest path to a successful customer loyalty initiative is through implementing a series of successful small changes over time.

As you shift, reinforce the changes you want implemented by using consistent internal communication. Team members want to know the goal they're working toward is still relevant. They need reassurance that the initiative won't be a flavor-of-the-month. And they need to know what's expected of them.

Reinforcement doesn't have to be drudgery. You can make it fun. One of my retail clients realized her employees didn't have sufficient product knowledge, and it was getting in the way of her loyalty initiatives. It also hurt sales when customers came into the stores and didn't receive good information about the products. She made product information available, but new merchandise came into the store on a daily basis. Motivating employees to invest in daily product knowledge updates was challenging. Her goal was getting employees to become more familiar with the products in order to improve revenue.

My client created a game in which team members earned points for knowing details about new merchandise. She created the rules and rewards, implemented the game, and made sure her managers played it with her salespeople in the store every day. Some of the rules were designed to bring out a sense of fun. Employees won regular prizes as their product knowledge increased. Over time, the team felt more connected to the stores, and customers noticed. Positive feedback to the managers increased and so did month-over-month sales.

One reason the game worked well was that the owner played, too. The team enjoyed more one-on-one interaction with her, which was an unexpected positive byproduct for everyone. When your team sees their leaders get involved achieving company goals, it demonstrates the goals' importance and reinforces consistency.

Track and Measure for Compliance, Course Correction, and Agile Improvement

Tracking and measuring results will help everyone on your team follow your clear guidelines for company culture. It's particularly valuable to track and measure the elements of culture that support customer loyalty, since that's your primary priority. Determine how to translate your expectations into quantifiable data and let your team know how they will be measured. Set them up for success because when they win, your culture wins, and your company wins.

Tracking and measuring also give you a clear metric to determine whether you're getting the compliance you've requested. Your team needs evidence that you're monitoring their compliance with your priorities. If they sense you're slacking, they'll be likely to slack as well. Just like your customer-facing initiatives, your company's culture is determined by what you do, not merely by what you say.

Reporting on progress is another way to keep the goal alive for your team. When they know you're paying attention to their progress, they'll be more motivated to engage. They'll also know their results are being watched. Team members tend to be more attentive to areas that receive obvious attention from the company's leaders.

Analyzing data enables you to stress-test objectives. Sometimes, you'll pick the wrong goals. Tracking and measurement provide data that helps you figure out whether you're on the right track. When you have this information, you can decide if or when to pivot.

Know what you want to measure and measure it. Be willing to change programs that don't work.

Square Capital's Jackie Reses says, "Know what you want to measure and measure it. Be willing to change programs that don't work. If you've created incentives that don't match what you're trying to reward, change them."

If you create an expectation for employees, it's important that you track what they do, measure their progress, and expect compliance. Following up to hold team members accountable doesn't have to be negative or involve terrible consequences. In fact, you can celebrate positive outcomes.

Add Celebration for Positive Reinforcement

One way to reinforce culture is to celebrate employees who model the behavior you want. Celebration shows your team that their actions matter. Millennial and Gen Z employees, in particular, gravitate to companies where they feel seen, heard, and valued as partners in contributing to company success. Employees of every generation are more inclined to be enthusiasts for customer-facing strategies when they feel appreciated.

Celebration doesn't have to be a big expense. For some employees, recognition of their actions can be a sufficient boost. Celebration is an opportunity for your company's leaders to demonstrate how much you prioritize a culture of engagement.

Reward team members who are doing well as a way to show your team you're paying attention to culture initiatives. The rewards you choose should be determined by your team's values. What works for some won't motivate others. Whether you create personalized rewards or one single, consistent celebration is up to you. Celebration is a fantastic way to show employees they're valued as contributors and ambassadors to customers.

For example, my retail client who created the product knowledge game added a semi-secret "caught being good" aspect to it. She invited key lucrative loyals to identify employees who were particularly well-versed in product knowledge and who shared that knowledge appropriately. This aspect of the game was a great way for her to involve the store's most engaged customers and have some fun.

When customers identified them, the employees received prizes, which varied in value. Some prizes, such as gift cards or recognition certificates, were awarded on the spot. These items might seem to be so small they wouldn't matter to employees, but they did. Employees loved the recognition and the goodies.

As an added bonus, the customers who were invited to "catch" employees "being good" loved being brought into a deeper relationship with the company. For these customers, being part of the activity reinforced their loyalty to the business.

That said, there are pitfalls to celebration. For example, if you choose to celebrate with a cake, you'll have to deal with the reality that one employee will be on a low-calorie diet, another will be gluten-free, and a third will inevitably have a philosophical issue with sugary snacks in the office. Some employers bail out of celebration initiatives due to these types of issues. Finding the right celebration might occasionally feel like a burden, but the upside of engaged employees, loyal customers, and a more productive business is worth the time and effort of finding a celebration that resonates with your team.

There are many positive opportunities for celebration. When tied to your customer loyalty goals, celebration becomes productive as well as enjoyable.

CASE STUDY: PERQ

PERQ is a marketing technology company that sells high-level con-sumer engagement for complex purchases, such as apartments and cars. Co-founders Andy Medley and Scott Hill deliberately manage an approach to culture that's geared toward consistent results. They have a lot of fun with a purpose.

The company uses a bullseye they call "the game of business."

"Officially, our mission is creating meaningful engagement be-tween consumers and brands," says Medley. "That's the reason why we exist as a business. But the touchstone of the 'game' is something we use internally as a guidepost. Our game includes a culture of en-gagement and respect that extends to our customers."

Says Hill, "We use 'the game' as a blueprint for a company where everyone is truly invested in trying to give their all and care about results."

"The game starts with transparent goals," Medley adds. "Every January we roll out the annual plan. We remind the team of the long-term mission and vision, and then we dive into our annual goals and how each department fits into the massive priorities we have for the organization. Each year, we pick three key goals.

"So that's the big picture, and everyone understands it. Every-body knows the revenue number we're trying to hit and the customer retention numbers that we're trying to hit. Next, we break that down into quarterly goals. Then the department leaders break down how each department's goals roll up to the overall quarterly goal. And then each employee has an individual score."

These are the measurable steps that stem from PERQ's clearly stated goals. PERQ then tracks and measures against those goals at the departmental and individual levels.

"Each department's and every individual's numbers are posted on scoreboards around the building," says Medley. "If we meet 100 percent of our annual goal on a quarterly basis, we incentivize it. If a department hits their quarterly goal, they get a half-day off. And if seven to ten departments hit their department's goals, it's another half-day off for everyone at the company. To get people to pay attention, we announce an update every month."

For some people, this culture of transparency and competition doesn't resonate. Those people either don't join the company or don't last at PERQ. For employees who stay, there's a lot of buy-in, in part because of the way the company manages the "game," using celebrations that employees choose to promote alignment with key initiatives.

Medley says, "If we hit those goals, the company wins prizes that enhance the office environment. There's an internal team that picks which prizes the company is playing for. Some of the things we've 'won' have been a high-end coffee bar, cereal bar, fruit stand, and soda machine. And we track those results transparently, too, updating the numbers each month."

Many of the core values the game celebrates are specifically and directly connected to the customer experience. One of the core values is actually called "customer value creation." By providing the game, PERQ consistently reinforces the importance of customer experience for its employees.

Hill and Medley insist they don't bring any special magic to the table, yet PERQ's numbers are impressive. In three years, the company has grown its cumulative annual growth rate by 900 percent. That represents a lot of loyal customers.

Hill says, "The company's ability to grow as fast as we have is a byproduct of the team understanding what we're trying to accomplish. The time we spend educating the team about our mission, direction, and strategy—and helping them understand their role in it—means they can run toward it faster. They can ask questions and challenge what we're doing, and that makes us better. More important, when people know their role and how it's connected to the big picture, we get the advantage of their whole brain being engaged, which ultimately means a better experience for customers."

CHAPTER 13

Use Data to Amplify Customer Value

When I was in business school, people joked about the difference between "poets" and "quant jocks." "Poets" dealt with people issues, such as management and marketing. (I was a proud poet.) The "quant jocks" respected data-driven number-crunching above all else. There was a friendly battle over which was more important. As it turns out, to cultivate loyalty, you need people *and* data; they are interrelated.

You begin with data. Data is information you gather to understand your customers so you can nurture those relationships. But data by itself is meaningless. It's raw material. Data only has value when you can use it effectively and consistently. That's where tracking and measuring play a role to extend loyalty. You need a system to track and measure to make data meaningful so you can take appropriate actions with customers.

Tracking and measuring are related but distinct. Tracking refers to the data you extract to tell a story about your customers. Your systems probably capture a lot of data. The value to your organization has less to do with collection and more to do with your ability to extract the information you need to track. To enhance customer loyalty, you only have to track a portion of that data. Too much can inhibit insights, so use only data you need to understand customers.

Measuring is the analysis of the information you track to yield actionable outcomes. Measurement takes the data you track and manipulates it to provide insights. Suppose you want to know if your customers are becoming more engaged with your company. You ask how you can identify increased customer engagement, and you decide that engaged customers are more likely to read your email messages. You filter your data to extract and track the rates at which your customers open your email messages. Those open rates are data. When you track that data over time and look at the trends, that's measurement. You use measurement to answer questions about loyalty by analyzing the data you tracked. The best approaches for tracking and measuring are consistent and applied systematically.

You make data meaningful by using it as a tool to understand your customers.

Can you identify your lucrative loyals without a system? Sure. You probably know business owners who are innately brilliant with people: they remember their customers' names, know what they've purchased, and inspire them to want more. While some small companies can feel their way to loyal customers with this ad hoc approach, it's not a system, and it doesn't scale, which limits the company's growth potential.

You make data meaningful by using it as a tool to understand your customers. To track and measure for loyalty, consider the questions about your customers that you want to answer. It's easier to figure out which data you need to track and measure when you're clear about what you want to know.

Recently, I worked with a client who provides membership services. The company brought me in to improve customer retention for a product that's purchased as an annual membership. The company was experiencing high levels of customer turnover and asked me to examine the communication sequence leading up to the membership renewal. The objective was to improve renewal rates for this product, and the question was, "How can we change the renewal conversation to improve our customer retention?"

I audited the process and asked my client for data that tied the customer retention problem to the renewal conversation. They couldn't provide this data, other than their low renewal rates. I had to dig further.

I discovered my client had made assumptions about its customers' behavior based on their problem, namely, the non-renewal. My client's goal of improving customer retention didn't align with the question they needed to answer. Instead of asking, "Why aren't customers renewing?" they asked themselves, "What's going wrong with our renewal conversation?" That question made an assumption the problem was with their renewal conversation. The assumption caused them to miss vital data.

When I looked at the data from their customer's perspective, I found the moment of disengagement was earlier. Much earlier.

In fact, the client was losing customers at the point of onboarding because the onboarding sequence didn't provide customers the tools they needed to be successful when they first bought the product. From the earliest days after they'd signed up, customers weren't invested in the company. By the time the renewal rolled around, any tenuous connection was long gone. A series of email messages and videos at the point of renewal wouldn't resurrect a relationship that had gone off the rails months earlier. The fundamental problem wasn't the renewal conversation, as my client initially assumed. By looking at the customer data, my client was able to shift the project's focus to the onboarding sequence.

My client wanted to improve retention rates. That's a clearly articulated goal, which is a necessary component for tracking data successfully. So far, so good. Where my client missed the mark was in using that goal to identify the question they wanted data to answer.

Asking, "What's wrong with our renewal conversation?" sent the effort down the wrong path. Had they continued in that direction, they would have spent more time and money trying to fix the wrong problem. Their effort wouldn't have produced results, and everyone would have been disappointed by the outcome.

Fortunately, discovery of the real problem allowed them to reframe their question and dig into the right data to determine why their onboarding process didn't cultivate the customer engagement that would lead to better renewals.

Once my client understood that their onboarding sequence triggered their customer retention problem, they needed to better understand the specific challenges their customers had during onboarding. They asked:

- What parts of the existing onboarding sequence worked?
- Which parts didn't work?
- At what point did customers lose interest?

We reframed those questions in ways that were data-driven and, therefore, could be tracked and measured. By asking, "What percentage of new customers opened the initial email messages?" we determined that tracking email open rates and measuring them over time would yield valuable information we could apply to solutions.

Similarly, the question, "What percentage of email recipients click through to get more information?" led us to examine email click-through rates.

We also determined that website usage would yield valuable data to answer questions about customer behavior. The client extracted data about the use of their web-based onboarding tools to look at customer behavior. Data also provided insight into how many times users logged into the website during the onboarding sequence and how many times customers returned to the client's onboarding tools.

Using this historical data, we tracked and measured a few key areas to examine past customer behavior. This provided insight into the actions customers had or hadn't taken during the onboarding, and that yielded clues into their level of engagement with the product and their subsequent renewal decisions.

By analyzing data from the onboarding sequence, my client made changes to two aspects of the customer experience. First, they created a campaign that sent an automated email message to every new member with a step-by-step guide to all of the benefits of membership. Then, the client created an online hub that explained their membership benefits. These resources made it easy for customers to get the onboarding information they needed and launch their membership successfully.

With improved outreach and the hub in place, my client saw immediate results. Not only did the new onboarding tools save more than one thousand hours of work each year, but the company also improved the email click-through rate for their onboarding sequence by 167 percent. At that rate, they expect to increase lifetime customer value by almost 400 percent. These two relatively small changes created huge results because they used data to pinpoint the exact issues that were blocking customer loyalty, and then they solved those problems to improve renewals.

Soapbox Revisited

Soapbox is another company that successfully used data to improve long-term customer loyalty. This consumer-packaged goods company's buyer is the commercial retailer that sells their product to customers. Soapbox can get some data from these retail partners, but they wanted additional customer information. In the past, Soapbox had relied on paid market research for insights into customer preferences. While that market research is valuable, it's expensive and not particularly agile. Plus, the artificial environment of market research doesn't always yield the same high-caliber results as looking at actual customer data. Soapbox asked, "How can we learn directly from our users?" That was their question.

Soapbox found a way to answer that question by using its social mission strategically to gather data. Every Soapbox product contains a "hope code," which the customer can enter into the Soapbox website to see where in the world the donation from their purchase was made.

The hope code provides a genuine point of connection for Soapbox's customers. Those who enter their code want to know where their aid was given. By entering their code, they get to know their purchase of the product made a difference.

CEO Dave Simnick says, "We get emails all the time from customers. They tell us it's meaningful to know their donation went to this or that location. One woman wrote and said, 'My donation went to [a town in India], and I've actually been there! It means a lot to me that I supported those people, thank you.' This connection reinforces customer loyalty to Soapbox."

The hope code also provides an important benefit for the company. When consumers enter their hope code, they share their name and email address so Soapbox can send an email message to them with the information about where their donation was sent. Of every customer who buys Soapbox products from mass retailers across America, ranging from Target and Walmart to Amazon and Walgreens, more than 1.5 percent of that significant number of customers enters their hope code. This feature yields a bounty of high-quality customer data.

With an email address, Soapbox can connect directly with these customers, sharing information about the company's products and promotions via a newsletter. Soapbox plans to add even more features for these folks, such as exclusive promotions for hope code users. The company can also tap these customers for feedback, product preferences, and more. In all these ways, the hope code allows Soapbox a mechanism to extract data to create deeper relationships with their customers.

Even better, it provides a way for the company to learn what inspires and excites their most engaged consumers.

As the company learns more about their best customers, they can tailor their products and promotions. Customers feel more seen, heard, and valued by Soapbox. Engagement with the hope code goes up. The process continues to be refined as more and more customers are inspired to enter their hope codes. Soapbox has developed a virtuous cycle of customer interaction.

Generate Data the Way You Need It

Companies use data successfully when they understand the problems they're trying to solve, frame questions so data can be applied to get answers, and then take action based on the insights from the data.

Understanding your customers relies on tracking and measuring data on an ongoing basis. Your system must generate the data you need in the way you want to analyze it and in a timeframe that suits your purposes.

Creating systems that spit out data so you can analyze it can mean capturing information in a variety of ways. One way to consistently analyze the data you measure is through reports. Some technology systems can generate reports automatically. For example, an email system typically can generate a monthly report of open rates and click-through rates.

At other times, your team might gather key data so you can assess it on a regular basis. My client couldn't extract website login data using a report that was automatically generated. This data had to be gathered manually by an employee each month.

Sometimes companies have to use a combination of automated and manual processes to get the data they need to trigger action. For example, a customer's quarterly business review might need both automated and manual processes. The system might automatically remind your team to schedule an end-of-quarter meeting, but reaching out to the customer and coordinating the people to attend the meeting is a manual step. Once the meeting takes place, employees might have to enter that data into the customer's system so there's a record of the activity. Data is always being collected. Clear communication about the goals you're trying to achieve will make it easier for your team members to build systems to track and measure the best possible data to produce loyal-ty-building results.

A lot of data is easy to collect. Where companies tend to falter is consistency. Leaders need to be clear in their expectations for ex-tracting and analyzing data on a regular basis. Knowing what you want to achieve, creating targeted systems to analyze the data you extract, and taking action based on what you learn is how you con-tinually improve customer connection.

Data is a story told with numbers.

It's more valuable to track fewer things successfully than to track a lot of information erratically. When data is used to build re-lationships, you get an opportunity for continuous improvement, which further improves loyalty. There's always something an orga-nization can do better to target loyalty. Your results will be driven by your efforts to act on the information you track and measure consistently.

Data is a story told with numbers. It uses technology, but it's ultimately about connection and human action.

CASE STUDY: ESPRIT DE LA FEMME

Cheryl Cote is the owner of Esprit de la Femme, an independent up-scale lingerie store that opened in 2002. When Cote applied the five factors to her business, data helped her grow her company during a time of relative contraction in the retail market.

"My customers desperately need what I offer," Cote says, "and the selling process takes time. There are a lot of variables in each lingerie purchase because we deal with each woman's unique body, and bra fitting is surprisingly technical. My team helps each customer individually to make sure they get exactly what they need and want.

"We noticed that some customers would suck up all of the expertise my team offered and then buy a cheaper bra elsewhere. Or they would go online and buy from someone who didn't offer the same level of service. Those online guys didn't have the training and expertise I offered, so they could undercut my prices. We spent time with customers only to have them buy from the bargain guy online after I had done all the hard work. I got sick of it.

"I decided to change things up and commit to building my business. I decided to invest in myself as a business owner and in my company. I started by focusing on what made my business special and what made people come back and shop with us again and again.

"I realized that people were buying us, not just our product. The product is everywhere. People have a choice. So I had to think about why they were choosing Esprit de la Femme when they could go anywhere they wanted, online or to another store.

"I can't be all things to all people, but I want to be the best for the people I serve. I created a clear profile of my top customer. I kept that profile in mind as I designed my customer experience process for the store. Keeping her clear in my mind made it very easy to be consistent. By being more narrowly focused, my voice got clearer.

"Even when I renovated the store, I was mindful of appealing to that woman. After the renovation, as I was buying inventory for the store, I kept asking myself what this customer would want. I didn't try to buy merchandise that would appeal to everyone, and the merchandise I chose had nothing to do with the customer's age or bra size. It had to do with an attitude.

"The biggest part of my store's transformation came from a computer program that tied inventory to customer profiles. I didn't want to invest the money, but the program meant I could see what customers were buying, even when I wasn't physically in the shop. I could see which parts of my inventory were working and which weren't, what brands were selling and at what price points. Now I can look at the report and know. Sometimes the information was right in front of my face, but I didn't realize what was happening until I had the computer and could see the reports.

"One brand I love was selling like hotcakes. Then, for whatever reason, it stopped. I didn't know what changed. The extra inventory was hanging in the store. Visually, it was in my face. But I kept ordering more. Once I had the computer system, I got a report, and when I looked at it, I said, 'Why do I have so much of this brand in stock?' Having the reports changed everything. It was all in black and white."

At Esprit de la Femme, having systems to track and measure inventory, profit margin, and customer purchases led directly to an improvement in customer retention rates. Margins went up because the store was better able to identify products that sell faster and at full price and items that needed to be discounted.

"Because of the information from the computer system, I know so much more about my customers," Cote says." Everyone on the team can help them so much better. Returns have dropped to next to nothing. And that's rare in retail. It's been a huge, huge turning point for me to see data that I hadn't seen before."

When Cheryl Cote began to implement the five factors at Esprit de la Femme, she began with a need to learn about her lucrative loyals. She didn't have a full database of customer information. In fact, her customer information was stored on index cards. Though primitive, it gave her a way to get in touch with her best customers.

Cote created a process to reach out to her best customers and offered them VIP appointments. She made these appointments top-notch, catering to an experience she knew her VIPs would appreciate. Whenever one of those customers came in, the staff followed clear steps for the VIP experience to ensure it was consistent from champagne to follow up. Through these VIP appointments, she was able to gather essential information, infuse cash, and stress test the value of investing in a systematic customer experience.

The VIP appointments were exclusive and by invitation only. While time-consuming, they produced the valuable insights she needed to refine the profile of her lucrative loyals. For Esprit de la Femme, the appointments were also something the store could do to jumpstart their loyalty initiative. And they were a big success. Within ninety days, the store achieved a 35 percent increase in revenue as a result of their direct outreach to VIP customers.

Over time, Cote's investments in people, process, and technology identified less time-intensive ways to cultivate the store's loyal customers. Changing priorities meant the VIP appointments were no longer the right fit for the business.

Today, Esprit de la Femme is evolving into a new era of customer loyalty with a points-based program that takes lucrative loyals into account. Cote says, "Everyone is welcome to the program, and VIPs get rewarded even more as they spend. Having a clear picture of our VIPs allowed us to get smarter about what makes them tick. We keep building our customer loyalty program one step at a time, and it's getting better and better."

Esprit de la Femme is located in Nelson, British Columbia, a western Canadian town of ten thousand people. How much upside could there be for a brick-and-mortar business in such a small town? The company began the process of actively cultivating loyalty five years ago. By the end of the first year, the company's revenue was up 25 percent year-over-year during an overall downturn for brick-and-mortar retail.

Five years later, Esprit de la Femme hasn't maintained a 25 percent gain. They've done much better. The store has enjoyed a revenue increase of 34 percent. That's a lot of happy customers. Customers come from all over western Canada to Nelson expressly to shop at the store.

Customers come back faster, spend more, and refer other customers like crazy. Employee tenure is up, and the team spirit is better than ever. It's a positive ripple effect that continuously expands outward. What's really amazing is that in the middle of the five-year span, Cote faced a potentially life-threatening illness. Most independent retailers wouldn't be able to weather that storm. With systems in place, backed by data Cote could monitor from home, Esprit de la Femme not only survived but thrived.

CHAPTER 14:

Use Feedback to Refine the Customer Experience

No matter what your company does, there's a human component to your customer relationships, and people are unpredictable. Employees screw up. Customers have complaints, both reasonable and unreasonable. Sometimes customers see a competing product or service and question their relationship with your company. Even the most loyal customers can be distracted by shiny things. It happens.

To stay ahead of potential problems, you have to listen to people's feedback about your company and use this feedback effectively. Whether it's Twitter, Yelp, or one of the many websites that want to become your industry's "Yelp for B2B," customers want to share their experiences. Not only that, but they also expect to get a response—and quickly. Research from the Local Search Association reveals that the majority of customers expect a company to respond to them within twenty-four hours.

Your effort to respond to customers in a timely manner pays off in the form of your company's online reputation. According to *Harvard Business Review*, responding to customer reviews improves online ratings.

Feedback is also a great way to learn about your customers. Any time you learn about your customers, and particularly your lucrative loyals, you improve your ability to understand them better and serve them more effectively. The more you show your customers that you're listening to them, the more they'll feel appreciated. This loop leads to even deeper loyalty, which motivates customers to buy more, stay longer, and refer additional customers. By understanding these deeply loyal customers better, you can make your advertising and product improvements more effective. You can earn more revenue and enjoy better margins. Using feedback effectively enhances the virtuous cycle of loyalty for your company.

When you've successfully cultivated loyalty, you earn customers who are so dedicated to your company that they want to share their thoughts with you. They root for your success and want to provide constructive ideas for improvement and even kudos. I'm a big fan of sending letters of appreciation to companies that have provided excellent customer experiences. I almost always receive an appreciative reply. As a result, I feel good, they feel good, and even when I initiated the letter, it reinforces my connection to the company.

Realistically, most feedback won't be positive. Whether positive or negative, it's in your best interest to respond to any feedback and acknowledge your customers' opinions. A system for feedback enables you to extract and evaluate what customers say about your company so you can employ their comments in ways that promote loyalty.

Extracting Feedback

Feedback can come from a formal process, such as a customer opinion survey. Feedback can also be obtained informally from customers who share feedback with your employees or through social media. Make no mistake, feedback about your company exists, and it's your job to listen and understand how your customers perceive their experience with your company.

Formal Feedback

There are many ways to get formal feedback. Sometimes, you'll want to ask for feedback to assess customers' reaction to new conditions, such as a new initiative, process, or product. Other times, you might ask customers for feedback about the same factors over time to explore their changing opinions about your customer experience. Surveys that ask customers for their opinions are a classic example of asking for feedback. In the last week, I've received email messages from companies asking my opinion about a trip I took, a potential product line expansion, and my experience calling customer support. People are asked for a lot of feedback, presumably to improve customer experience.

When you ask for feedback and then you don't use it, it's insulting. Building relationships means being considerate. If you ask customers to provide feedback, you should show respect for their time by using the information they provide.

Since customers get asked for a lot of feedback, you'll want to be thoughtful about any requests you make. When using feedback to enhance loyalty, you might not want to ask every customer for their opinions. Instead, develop a plan to use the feedback before you ask for it so you can clarify how you'll frame your requests and whom you'll ask. You might want to focus your requests on the customers whose opinions you value most, your lucrative loyals. Lucrative loyals will have opinions about your company. When those opinions skew negative, it will always be better if your loyals share those opinions directly with you, rather than out in the world. Provide your loyals with a clear path to send feedback so you can evaluate it and respond.

You're most likely to receive meaningful feedback when you have a process that builds connectedness. This process begins with a sincere desire to hear what customers have to say. We've all received surveys that state, "We value your feedback." How often do you actually feel valued by that statement? The more customers feel seen, heard, and valued as individuals, the more committed they will be to providing helpful feedback.

You're most likely to receive meaningful feedback when you have a process that builds connectedness.

To make formal feedback valuable, consider how you'll ensure unbiased opinions. You won't learn anything actionable if your feedback data is skewed from the outset. Car salespeople are notorious for aggressively attempting to direct the satisfaction scores customers provide after they buy a new car. When I bought a new car recently, my salesman said, "If I get anything less than all tens, it's a huge problem for me. I could lose my job. I'm going to give you this survey, but you have to give me all tens, OK?" Management won't learn any valuable information from that exercise.

Your process to extract feedback has to be based on your sincere interest in what customers have to contribute.

A regular process for talking to customers and hearing their direct input is useful. Asking for formal feedback from customers is a whole-company job that begins with the company's leaders. Everyone, starting with the CEO, should have an opportunity and be required to engage directly with your customers.

Companies have been successful engaging customers with goals. For example, a customer advisory board can be a great way to get actionable feedback. It can be difficult to ask customers to advise your company, but the right customers will be enthusiastic about your success, and having a formal role can magnify their loyalty. Whether you use a formal advisory board, informal coffee klatch, or hired third-party to get insights, feedback from your lucrative loyals can help to ensure your initiatives aim for your bullseye.

Informal Feedback

With social media, it's easier than ever for customers to share informal feedback about their experiences with your company. Feedback is often generated after some aspect of a customer's experience, such as:

- Specific information about an interaction with an employee.
- Customers' observations about your facilities or their experiences with your company.
- Opinions about your products or services.

Informal feedback is more likely to be negative. This isn't universally true, but it's the odd-on favorite. Getting negative feedback might not be fun, but it has value for cultivating loyalty.

A single complaint generally indicates a larger problem because most unhappy customers don't bother to tell the company about their bad experience. Research reveals that for every customer who complains, twenty-six more who are also unhappy leave and never come back to tell you why they left.

It can be useful to think about customers who voice their complaints as icebergs. From the surface, an iceberg might look harmless, but beneath the water lies its bulk and what you can't see can be deadly. The same is true with unhappy customers. Even when you get only one or two complaints, chances are good there's a mass of dissatisfied customers under that visible tip.

Fortunately, social media offers an important upside to your ability to access and respond to informal customer feedback. Increasingly powerful tools, such as Hootsuite, enable companies to effectively hear what customers have to say. These tools can provide a wealth of insight.

When it comes to informal feedback, listening is the first way to improve loyalty. Your timely response creates a richer process to extend the conversation with customers so they feel seen, heard, and valued. Whether feedback is shared online or in person, employees need a clear process to capture and save feedback so it can be evaluated. If the process makes it easy for team members to gather feedback, they will be more likely to capture it for evaluation. When feedback isn't captured immediately, it's more likely to vaporize.

Once feedback is lost, everyone loses. Customers don't feel heard. Employees are frustrated because they have no constructive way to share feedback that could help the company. The company misses the lessons from that feedback.

Your team is your conduit to this vital information. Consider implementing ways to recognize and celebrate team members who follow directives for capturing feedback. Having a clear process to extract feedback treats it like the gift that it is.

Evaluate Feedback

Once you've captured customer feedback, whether it's formal or informal, the next move is to evaluate it and use it to improve loyalty. In some cases, feedback requires little more than an empathetic reply to the customer. Responding to feedback can be sufficient in some cases, especially when the feedback is positive. Customers like knowing their appreciation has been recognized.

In other situations, a response should include some specific next actions the customer can take, such as calling tech support or trying specific troubleshooting methods, to resolve the customer's problem quickly.

Occasionally, customer feedback suggests the company should employ a more hands-on approach to help that customer resolve their problem. In those cases, team members need a clear way to evaluate a complaint so they know how they're supposed to respond.

Just because a customer voices a complaint doesn't mean you should jump into making changes to your company. Before you take action, consider the source. All feedback is not equal. Focus on making shifts based on feedback that's aligned with your bullseye. Too often, when customers complain, companies react to the squeaky wheels. When you use feedback to improve customer loyalty, your decision to act on feedback should be strategic and should take lucrative loyals into consideration first.

The other day I received a phone call from a client whose company sells online training programs. He was nervous because a promotion he launched triggered an aggressively negative response from a customer. Based on the feedback, he was ready to change the promotion's marketing message and even considered pulling the plug on the promotion.

With a little conversation, we were able to ascertain that the customer who complained didn't fit the profile of my client's lucrative loyals. In fact, his loyal cohort had a positive response to his promotion.

The customer whose response was negative needed to be heard, but the company wouldn't have been well-served to pivot based on that customer's input. My client sent a caring email message to the customer, expressing appreciation for the feedback, but the promotion, appropriately, stayed on course.

Without knowing whom to listen to, it's difficult to know how to engage with feedback appropriately. That's one more reason it's vitally important to identify your lucrative loyals. Your ability to evaluate feedback through the lens of loyalty makes it easier to employ decisions to take action.

Use Your Feedback

In theory, feedback could let you know your company was doing everything well. You could learn that you should stay the course and change nothing. This situation is the kind of rare that makes people want to believe in unicorns. Most of the time, feedback offers you insight into a customer's desire for you to change something about your business.

When you evaluate feedback through the lens of loyalty, you might decide to act based on that information. When you decide to act based on feedback, there are internal and external elements to employ.

Internally, make sure any changes are communicated to your team so they're aware of them. If the changes require a new way for team members to engage with customers, activate your processes to train, track, and recognize team members' activities so that they have the support they need to enact the new procedures.

Externally, reconnect with the customers who shared the feedback with you. You can set yourself apart from your competitors by expressing your thanks and, when appropriate, sharing what you learned from your customers' insight. When you show appreciation for your customers' time and energy on your behalf, you demonstrate that your customers are seen, heard, and valued.

Feedback and Disruption

A special kind of feedback that requires particular attention is the indication of industry disruption. If your industry experiences seismic shifts, you have to decide how and when to adapt to changes that affect your company. Pivot too early and you can risk losing customers who aren't ready. Pivot too late and you can lose the whole ballgame.

So, how should you engage with disruption?

Disruption can make your relationship with loyal customers tricky to navigate. The customers who have been most loyal might not want your company to adopt an industry's new direction. Dedicated customers who have been profitable for your company might prefer stasis to change. These customers might resist a disruptive innovation. In these cases, listening to your loyals could be catastrophic to your company's future growth.

This scenario is precisely why customer lifetime value is a forward-looking metric. The customers who brought your company to where you are might not be the same customers who will take your company where you want to go. That's why you must constantly evaluate and re-evaluate your definition of lucrative loyals. Market disruption could shift the characteristics that put certain customers in your lucrative loyal cohort. In a disrupted market, you won't keep every loyal customer you have. Active evaluation means you'll have to make decisions about the customers you'll continue to prioritize as loyals.

How you manage the pivot will have a significant impact on your relationship with those customers. Some companies decide there's more value in staying the course and serving a smaller group of deeply loyal customers. Other companies determine that survival might mean shifting away from a previously loyal base. If your company chooses a new definition of lucrative loyals, be prepared for the negative feedback you'll likely get from customers you've served successfully in the past.

You might not make those customers happy, but you can get ahead of the problem with a thoughtful and caring message about the new direction your company will take. Communicate clearly and vigilantly monitor feedback to manage any fallout from your decision.

Even when you make changes that your past customers might not prefer, you can develop messages and feedback strategies that show respect for customers who have been loyal in the past. If and when you shift away from your lucrative loyals, celebrate your journey with them by showing how much you've valued the relationship.

Fortunately, disrupted markets are the exception, not the rule, for feedback. Generally, your process to manage formal and informal feedback effectively will emphasize consistent active listening so you can respond in ways that demonstrate commitment to your customers.

PART V

Putting It All Together

This section of this book is tactical. We'll cover how to put every-thing together to make loyalty your everyday reality with a three-step plan:

- Step I: Analyze your existing conditions to discover what your company needs to succeed.
- Step II: Create an action plan that gets your team members engaged with your customer loyalty initiative.
- Step III: Launch and nurture your initiative for long-term success.

CHAPTER 15

Step I: Uncover Your Company's Issues and Opportunities

C ustomer loyalty is a process that marries emotional connection with consistent systems for implementation. The threads of heart and smart are interwoven through the fabric of your company's customer experience.

When a company is ready to enjoy the benefits of loyalty, they need to take action. But action without a plan is unlikely to produce great results. The rewards of cultivating loyalty are worthy of taking the time to aim before you fire.

How you implement this in your company will naturally vary based on the size of your company and your company's existing process for clear, consistent customer experience. Don't be overwhelmed by steps that are beyond your company's current capacity. Adding any consistent process for customer experience will generate positive results, so rightsize your action plan to the steps your company can implement successfully.

Begin with an evaluation of the existing conditions in your organization. That means taking a clear-eyed look at the way your company is currently structured for loyalty, the challenges you're facing, and the opportunities ahead.

The rewards of cultivating loyalty are worthy of taking the time to aim before you fire.

Two approaches that I generally recommend to evaluate your company's existing situation are an assessment or an audit.

Use Assessments for High-Level Understanding of Your Company

An assessment asks people on your team a consistent series of questions about your company's current orientation to customer loyalty. Assessments are relatively quick and effective ways of gathering information. The process is straightforward and cost effective.

Comparing responses gives you an idea of the current reality. An additional benefit is that an assessment engages a number of people inside your company. When you begin your process by including team members, they'll be primed from the beginning to buy into your initiative later on. People appreciate feeling their experience counts. Once an organization decides to make changes, their buy-in will make change easier.

To ensure honest responses, it's helpful to have an objective third-party ask your team members how your company engages with customers. When assessments are evaluated by an outsider, there's more opportunity for respondents to remain anonymous, which allows your team members to share their thoughts without the risk of attribution.

The output of an assessment acts as a report card that evaluates your existing conditions for customer loyalty so you can identify key opportunities for improvement.

Use Audits for a Tailored Examination of Your Existing Process

An audit is a customized approach to analyzing the existing conditions inside your company. Instead of a consistent series of questions, an audit investigates your existing process to engage loyal customers. An audit explores your company's specific process to inspire customers and investigates how your company is set up to cultivate loyalty.

Audits generally look at a company's existing people, processes, and technologies, both internally and externally. Audits provide an understanding of areas where a company excels, where they lag, and what's required to bridge the gaps.

Unlike assessments, which follow a consistent process, audits vary from company to company to provide a tailored map. An audit might include a kickoff meeting, team interviews, and an evaluation of your company's customer experience, marketing, and internal practices. Audits often include conversations with current and former customers to understand the experience from their perspective.

It's generally helpful to have an audit performed by someone outside the company. A third-party ensures objectivity, which can be hard to achieve when internal team members perform the audit. Insiders may be inadvertently blind to biases or assumptions in an organization. Plus, it's generally harder for people inside the company to deliver bad news. You don't want your report to undermine what the audit discovers.

The outcome of an audit presents findings that are specific to the company. Findings might include:

- Interview findings.
- Map of existing conditions.
- Gap analysis that compares existing conditions with your ideal state.
- Roadmap of potential next actions.
- Opportunities for additional revenue streams, if identified.
- Additional opportunities for improvement in people, processes, and technologies to enhance the customer experience.

Assessments and audits can be valuable tools for identifying current conditions to identify the company's most lucrative opportunities for improvement. An assessment is faster and less expensive but doesn't explore your company's unique approach to customer loyalty. An audit is costlier than an assessment because it's a more in-depth and customized approach.

CHAPTER 16:

Step II: Launch Your Loyalty Initiative

O nce you've evaluated your existing conditions, it's time to move into action so your company can launch your loyalty initiative.

Develop Your Bullseye Message

Implementation begins with having your company's leaders gather to decide which specific area of focus you'll choose to launch first. This is the time to hold your bullseye workshop.

In the bullseye workshop, your team's key decision-makers will lay out your rings of connection, as covered in chapter 5. These rings assess your company's foundational elements, features and benefits, value, and personal improvement. Then your group will tie those rings to the specific emotion your company wants your customers to feel so they are seen, heard, and valued.

You'll then draft a bullseye message and let the workshop attendees try to tear it apart. You're looking for a message that will work for your company in all circumstances. With a little tailoring to fit your company's culture and some creativity and buy-in, a bullseye message is born. Your bullseye will become the gold-standard for talking about customer experience inside your company as the message your team members use to guide their customer interactions.

Create Your Roadmap

Once the bullseye message is in place, look at the results of your company's assessment or audit to identify the areas of implementation you'll use to launch your loyalty initiative. In all likelihood, your evaluation will have identified a number of opportunities for your company. Enthusiasm may exist to tackle all of them, but you can't do everything at once. In fact, it's counterproductive.

Implementing changes with a series of two-degree shifts will be more effective in the long term.

Implementing changes with a series of two-degree shifts that get introduced in phases will be easier for team members to manage and more effective in the long term. It takes time for change to take root, and team members need an opportunity to digest training and new procedures. Ultimately, to effect long-term loyalty, trying to do too much too quickly can be the enemy of success. It's better to go slow and drip phased achievement into your organization than to go fast and undermine consistency.

At this point, it's helpful for your leadership team to pause and make sure all company leaders are on board with your initiative. If there are concerns or if your executives aren't in alignment, it's better to deal with it now. Launching loyalty needs a united front when you unveil the initiative to your team. Move forward when you have buy-in for your roadmap across your leadership team.

Convene a Taskforce

Launching your customer loyalty initiative will require a process to take you from idea to execution. Now is the time to involve team members in the launch process by convening a small, cross-functional taskforce that represents a number of departments and skillsets across the company. The taskforce can be made up of employees, external team members—such as freelancers or vendors—and a designated project leader.

The taskforce leader can be the CEO, the person your company designated to be responsible for customer experience, or someone else. Whoever leads the effort must have enough authority to direct change, allocate resources, and hold other taskforce members accountable. If the person in charge of the effort isn't a top-level leader, they will also need the full-throated, ongoing support of leadership.

An external advisor can also be an asset for your taskforce. An advisor provides the support to keep your group on track and the experience to safeguard against pitfalls. An advisor adds an objective perspective so the taskforce avoids the inclination toward insider thinking about the challenges of implementing loyalty. An impartial taskforce advisor can see what's possible and hold the group accountable in ways that can be difficult among peers. An advisor can also push back against any unreasonable leadership expectations in a way that's hard for a group of employees to do. That said, while an advisor can be an excellent guide, customer loyalty for the long term ultimately depends on your team to ensure consistent action, so the taskforce should be led not by the advisor but by someone inside your company.

The taskforce's initial job will be to identify and complete the required tasks to launch your loyalty initiative company-wide. A major pre-launch job for the taskforce will be to create a bullseye book, which is a reference that team members can use to remind themselves of what your bullseye message is, how it's used, and how it applies to them. The bullseye book will explain that the language of the bullseye message is for internal use. The bullseye informs the customer experience but isn't an external marketing message.

Launch Your Initiative

The big announcement to launch your loyalty initiative is ideally done in person at an all-hands meeting. Company-wide webinars or video conferences are fine, but they're not as effective as live interaction. Plus, a live launch shows everyone that your company takes the loyalty initiative seriously. Begin by having company leaders share your clear goals and explain how the initiative will improve the company and affect employees' work. Team members will engage more effectively when they feel confident there's a clear plan in place.

My clients have included some or all of the following elements in their successful launch events:

- Futurecast: Begin the announcement by sharing leadership's customer loyalty vision for the company. This is your story in which customers feel so valued that they become long-term lucrative loyals who buy more, stay longer, and refer new customers like crazy. The Futurecast expounds on the ways your company will grow and why that growth benefits everyone.

- Employee perspective: Illuminate the value of your company's future for your team members. As you make the announcement, team members will be focused on processing the information from their own perspective. They'll be wondering:

  ◦ Will this initiative actually happen? Or will it fizzle?

  ◦ What does this initiative mean for me and my workload?

  ◦ How can I be successful?

  ◦ How does this initiative benefit me?

  By explicitly incorporating employee-focused information, you'll show team members that you're considering their futures, as well the company's. You'll bring them into your vision. Be mindful of the questions they might have about their understandably self-interested roles. By prioritizing their perspective upfront, you'll show that you see, hear, and value your team. They'll be more likely to embrace the information you present once they believe their needs are an important part of the plan.

- Leadership's support: Make clear that this initiative is a priority of your company's leaders. Team members need to know that the direction comes from the top of the organization, that it will mean long-term change, and that you expect them to adhere to the plan.

- Taskforce validation: After company leaders explain that the project is a priority, they should also validate the taskforce. Everyone involved needs to know the members of the taskforce have worked hard to bring new ideas and work patterns to the company. This part of the announcement helps to empower the taskforce with authority to act.

- The bullseye message: The introduction of the bullseye message is a big "ta-da" moment. A little finesse builds drama for it. Your company will live and breathe your bullseye. In addition to explaining what it is and how it will be used to inspire customer loyalty, the announcement moment deserves a little flair.

- More about employees: Circle back to the employee experience so your team members know how the information will affect their jobs, starting with the training they'll receive. The more you manage expectations and build trust in the process, the easier it will be to motivate your team.

- Implementation milestones: Share the initial two-degree shifts you plan to take toward your big vision and any immediate changes you plan to make. Team members should walk away from the launch with a sense that there will be a process for change, that the changes will be in place for the long term, and that change will be introduced through a digestible process.

- Share your bullseye book: Your launch should also include distribution of the bullseye book your taskforce created to articulate the meaning and usage of your bullseye message. You don't want to rely on your employees' memories of the announcement. Have something available as a tangible resource to help spur immediate action, even if the resource itself is primarily virtual. The book should be available to all team members, not just employees, so you can speed the adoption of consistent bullseye messaging for everyone who engages with customers on behalf your company.

- Q&A: Allow time for your team members to ask questions, and also recognize that more questions might arise later. Provide a way for people to ask questions after the event so your team can stay focused during the launch.

- First action initiation: People feel more invested in a process when they've personally put effort into its success, so give your team members an explicit first action to take immediately. Even a small act will trigger that sense of connection. A quick exercise can accomplish this objective, ideally one where people commit to their first action in front of the team. For example, you can set up a big board and ask your team members to write one way they can use the bullseye message. This exercise might seem corny, but its power comes from having your team members take an action publicly in support of the initiative. Whatever first action you choose to do, include that at your launch event so team members walk away having already engaged in your process.

- Celebration: As you wrap up the launch presentation, mark the announcement with a celebration. Do something that's tied to your bullseye and pure fun to mark the occasion of the launch. Be mindful to choose a celebration that everyone can enjoy. Think of ways your celebration can be inclusive, festive, and an embodiment of your bullseye's spirit. Your advisor can help you come up with ideas.

CHAPTER 17

Step III: Make Lucrative Loyalty Your New Normal

Following your launch, the work of implementing your loyalty initiative will be directed by the person in charge of the customer experience. They might tap taskforce members for help as they calculate customer lifetime value, design necessary training for the initiative, and begin the first series of two-degree shifts.

Executives might need to reiterate the plan or add their support. Your leaders' unwavering support of the customer experience will ensure there's clear communication about its importance to the company while providing the gravitas and authority the lead person needs to act effectively.

Identify Your Lucrative Loyals

Next, lay out what it means to be a customer in your company's environment. This process begins with developing a future-looking assessment of customer lifetime value. Understanding your universe of customers, determine the characteristics that identify your lucrative loyals, limited loyals, lazy loyals, and average customers and decide how your company will trigger an ongoing assessment of customer lifetime value. It's tempting to create complex schemes to assess and reassess a customer's orientation to loyalty. Resist that temptation in favor of identifying the simplest possible way to classify loyalty.

Many departments will play a part in understanding and updating your company's customer lifetime value tracking and measuring, so everyone will need a clear understanding of what's expected of them and any new data they'll need to collect.

Training

Whether your company is large, medium, or small, team members will need training to reinforce new expectations for their actions. Define the scope of training and how to allocate training between formal and informal settings.

Formal training happens when you set aside time specifically to share and reinforce information. The all-hands launch of your loyalty initiative is the first stage of formal training because you gather your team expressly to announce and define the loyalty initiative. Additional formal training will likely follow the launch. This training might include seminars, workshops, or other coaching sessions dedicated to helping team members work with a bullseye and understand their role in the initiative.

If your company decides to change the way team members engage with customers, you'll want to include formal training for the new expectations. If new or changed procedures will be adopted to capture and use data, identify the best way to convey that technical information through formal training.

Formal training is generally the shorter and more straightforward part of launching a customer loyalty initiative. The longer and more complex part of embedding change in your organization comes from ongoing informal training. Informal training is the day-to-day reinforcement of the messages you're knitting into the fabric of the company.

Informal training involves consistently reminding team members about the bullseye message: why it matters, how it affects the company, and how every employee is tied to the initiative. Informal training doesn't have to be complex. It can be as simple as beginning every team meeting by reminding everyone what the goals for loyalty are. Continuous reinforcement helps to ensure that everyone aims for the same target.

In my experience, informal training is where companies tend to shortchange their efforts, turning a good strategic foundation into a flavor-of-the-month outcome. Whoever is in charge of the customer experience will need resources to implement a rightsized approach to formal and informal training over time to ensure that expectations are reinforced after the initial launch.

Ongoing Implementation

Next, your company will initiate the series of two-degree shifts previously identified by your leadership team. The specific projects your company undertakes at this point will be based on your company's unique needs. The universal goal for implementation is to keep it fast and flexible. An iterative approach allows your company to understand changing needs that arise in your customer relationships so you can adjust and take action. By structuring the taskforce this way, you create a more agile approach to loyalty and better position your company to address shifts as they arise.

Additional areas to consider:

- Designing the customer lifecycle from your company's first interaction with a prospect through the initial purchase, welcome, onboarding, upsells, inflection points, and any loyalty or rewards programs.

- Creating onboarding sequences that ensure new employees are embedded immediately into the company's initiatives. Employees who join the company after the initial launch need a fair opportunity to be equally successful cultivating loyalty.

- Creating ongoing interaction with customers, including guidelines for communication in alignment with your bullseye, internally and externally.

Many of my clients develop rules for customer-facing email messages and other communications. For example, a consistent salutation and sign-off for every email message might use "Hi" and the customer's first name instead of a formal honorific and the customer's surname. These details provide consistency that customers might not overtly notice but will subconsciously improve their trust in your company. Similarly, if the company runs a promotion, every customer-facing email message should use a standardized voice or image.

Add Recognition and Celebration to the Mix

Create an initial plan for customer recognition and celebration. Sometimes team members don't understand what recognition and celebration are or what a rightsized reward should be in a given situation. When celebration is a new concept, the taskforce may require some assistance to generate ideas, which your advisor can help you develop.

Your plan might include a list of customer actions with specific recognition and celebration outcomes and special consideration for customers who are, or show potential to become, lucrative loyals. Identify ways to recognize and celebrate team members who are cheerleaders for the process of cultivating loyalty. Celebration of team members who support your goals is a great way to reinforce positive expectations in your company.

Identify Technology Needs

Oftentimes, a company's customer loyalty plan requires changes to existing technology. When the timing is appropriate, investigate ways technology can support your initiative. It's not necessarily their job to solve the problems but rather to understand the human side of the customer experience that will be improved technologically.

Questions to consider might include:

- When a new customer comes onboard, how will key employees be reminded to activate the welcome and onboarding process?
- When a customer's regularly scheduled business review date is coming up, how will employees involved in that process be cued for action?
- When a customer starts to spend more or shows characteristics of loyalty, how will the team be alerted to that information?

Technology is also important to gather and assess feedback, track and measure data, and evaluate customer segments. Your customer data systems should store critical information, deliver reports, and cue team members to take actions that inspire, reward, and celebrate loyalty.

Decide how technology will track and measure the important data points that will be used to understand customer loyalty. While this process may seem daunting, it can be simplified at the outset. Strategic use of technology can enhance your efforts, but it's also an area where companies often get overwhelmed. Shifts in technology can take a lot of time. To maintain momentum, begin your process by finding creative ways to take incremental, if imperfect, action using the technology you have in place. Your goal is to be agile so your company can identify shifting needs and respond quickly. Once you've launched your customer loyalty initiative and have made needed tweaks, then consider adding or adjusting your technology.

Your goal is to be agile so the company can identify shifting needs and respond quickly.

Create a simple plan for people, processes, and technology. What might seem like a lot of steps is often distilled to a few vital activities that focus on your identified two-degree shifts. You're aiming for a smooth rollout of your loyalty initiative to your entire company and your customers.

Nurture Your Initiative for Long-Term Success

As you implement your plan, you invariably refine your approach to customer loyalty. These adjustments are part of the process. Your company and its leaders should be willing to hear your team's suggestions to alter goals when they're presented with reasonable and specific feedback to improve the process. Listening to suggestions is another way to make team members feel appreciated so they'll be ready and willing to provide your customers a superior experience.

Finding additional ways to celebrate achievement of incremental goals will help spur forward progress. Celebrations can be quick and free. They also should be tailored to your team's preferences. Some teams are motivated by banging a gong when milestones are reached. Others find that approach painful and cliched. Some teams may enjoy the gong for a while and then get tired of it. As long as celebrations are legal and appropriate, there are few right or wrong ideas. Celebrations succeed when they're meaningful and motivating for your team.

Shift toward Ongoing Support within a Working Group

After you launch your loyalty initiative, it's helpful to have your customer experience leader and key taskforce members meet periodically to discuss progress, consider pivots, and analyze the metrics of loyalty.

My clients often find it helpful to have a group that meets monthly or quarterly to discuss the company's ongoing customer loyalty goals. These meetings help the company ensure the effort remains active and vital without falling into the dreaded flavor-of-the-month vortex.

In these meetings, facilitated by your advisor or the person in charge of customer experience, the group talks about the implementation timeline and goals. They tackle accountability and troubleshooting. The facilitator should have the expertise and authority to guide the process, ease communication with company leaders, and ensure the loyalty initiative continues to move forward.

Some companies choose to have in-house groups manage this ongoing implementation within their company's environment. Others prefer a mastermind model where the customer experience leader joins employees of other companies who are managing similar customer-related processes. These mastermind groups offer ongoing training and support for your loyalty goals. They provide peer-to-peer advice and a forum to hear how other companies found success or learned from their mistakes.

Whether in-house or as part of a mastermind, your company's loyalty initiative will thrive when it gets ongoing attention and assistance.

CHAPTER 18

Take Your First Action

Your company taps into the heart and smart of customer loyalty by creating a consistent process for making customers feel seen, heard, and valued. When you're successful, you generate positive financial, strategic, and cultural impact for your company. You serve your customers, employees, team members, and leaders at a deeper level. The transactional customer experience becomes transformational.

You can get access to free resources to improve customer and employee loyalty in your company at:

www.keepyourcustomersbook.com/resources

The key to your success lies in a customer experience that inspires emotional connection.

Emotional connection allows you to develop customers who stay with you longer, buy more, and refer new customers. With emotional connection, you'll develop engaged employees. You will set your company apart from its competitors by knowing exactly how to find and retain lucrative loyalty.

This is your moment to decide that lucrative loyalty is your priority.

You can begin right here, right now.

Your journey begins with a decision to prioritize the heart and smart of loyalty.

Mark your decision by taking overt action.

Write down your commitment to customers on a post-it note and stick it somewhere you'll see it.

Tell a colleague.

Call a meeting.

Phone a friend.

Make a vision board.

You can even email me (ali@youriconicbrand.com) or find me on social media. I'll reply.

The people you serve are worth the effort, and your company deserves nothing less. Now is the time to keep your customers.

ACKNOWLEDGEMENTS

Writing a book isn't nearly as sexy as you might imagine: less soulful, deep thinking at charming cafes and a lot more angst. Birthing a book is a labor of love. Even more, it's a team effort, and I have been incredibly fortunate for the support of amazing people.

To start, this book is made infinitely better by the inspiring business leaders who shared their stories with me. I'm grateful for the thoughtful contributions of Chris Baggott, Cheryl Cote, Scott Hill, Ajay Kori, Andy Medley, Kara Nortman, Jackie Reses, Jeff Sheely, Dave Simnick, Mark Suster, and Craig Wedren.

When I was at Wharton, I got to learn from the incredible Pete Fader, and we have stayed in touch over the years. In addition to his big brain, I thank him for putting me in touch with Dan McCarthy. Dan's research at Emory was being published as the book was written, and it perfectly highlights the financial value of customer loyalty.

I had fangirled Kay Koplovitz long before meeting her for the first time when I was in college. She is one of the true pioneers of women leaders in business. The fact that she has written the foreword for this book still makes me giddy.

There are a few people without whom this book would not have been published. Marcie Geffner, editor extraordinaire, took the mess that was my first draft and guided me to a much tighter narrative. We all—*all*—owe her a big debt of gratitude. Huge thanks also to the amazing Jennifer Hanchey, who polished the final manuscript.

I've been incredibly lucky to have friends and colleagues who dedicated time and effort with perceptive feedback on the many drafts that eventually became this book. A special shout out to Jenni Edwards Burton, who went above and beyond with sage editing. Tim Conder, Stephan Cox, Ana Eccles, Kate Elliott, Marc Hertz, Aimee Kandrac, Susan Lassiter-Lyons, Lisa Silverman Meyers, Valory Myers, Joanna Schwartz, Teddy Shapiro, and Mara Winters were also helpful and generous with their feedback, and the book is better for it.

Jenni Robbins, who is equally a friend and trusted business advisor, introduced me to Morgan James Publishing. Thanks to Gayle West, David Hancock, Jim Howard, and Nickcole Watkins for your support and advice.

In addition to his fantastic contributions throughout the process of writing this book, Tim Conder has been an amazing and encouraging friend, sounding board, and strategist. Susan Rozzi has helped me keep my head on straight and stay focused.

To everyone on the Your Iconic Brand team, your dedication to our bullseye is fun and motivating. To Andrew Curtis and the FuelVM team, thank you for everything you do to make Your Iconic Brand's promise match its visual branding reality. You all rock.

To the Roundtable of Vixens, especially Ana, Ouisa, Tania, and Mega. It's hard to boil so many years of friendship into a pithy sentence or two, but I'm eternally appreciative for our continued adventures and our freaking fabulous group chat.

Growing up, my dad seemed to know everything and everybody. He always "had a guy" to help in any situation. Rules didn't always apply to my dad, and it took me a long time to understand why. It wasn't (as one of my early bosses mused) because he was somehow connected to a shady underworld. It was because he was an authentically great relationship builder. His example taught me how to be a good customer *and* cultivate loyalty. I only wish he was still with us to see how his influence is manifested in this book. I also know my mom would be proud of the achievement of writing this book.

I don't know who I would be in this world without my brother, Teddy Shapiro. If you're lucky enough to have a truly awesome sibling in your life, you know what I mean. If you don't, there are no words to express it. I just know I'm thankful. I'm also fortunate to have an insanely smart, thoughtful, loving sister-in-law in Joanna Schwartz.

To my kids, Charleigh and Christian, I love you both very much. I won the in-law lottery when it came to Carol and David Cudby and Tess and Jonathan Wisbey. To my fabulous niece, Kate Shapiro, and my equally amazeballs nephews, Julian Shapiro, Henry Wisbey, and Ollie Joe Wisbey, I adore our time together.

To Joe, wow. Literally, as I was typing this sentence, the doorbell rang and "just cuz" flowers were delivered. Damn, you're good. I'm grateful every day that I decided to take a cooking class. I'm lucky every day I get to be your partner in the adventure of life. As the title of our wedding song said, my aphrodisiac is you. Always.

And finally, a heartfelt thank you to the unknown saleswoman who helped me in the dressing room at Bravissimo many years ago. That transformational bra fitting started the zigzagging (yet uplifting) journey that ultimately inspired this book.

KEEP CONNECTED AND
YOUR BONUS MATERIAL

Thank you for reading! I want to make sure you get the most up-to-date ways to keep your customer, so check out your bonus material at:

www.keepyourcustomersbook.com/resources

Come find me at www.youriconicbrand.com. I'm also on Twitter (@alicudby) and LinkedIn (https://www.linkedin.com/in/alicudby/).

Finally, I have one small request. My customers love getting real-world customer experience stories in my blog posts. Some are inspiring, some are disastrous – all of them provide good lessons. If you have stories to share, please send them my way. Any feedback, questions or ideas are also welcome.

Email connect@youriconicbrand.com and you'll get a personal response.

I look forward to staying connected,

Ali

ABOUT THE AUTHOR: ALI CUDBY

Ali Cudby first cut her teeth in the world of customer experience after graduating from the Wharton School and joining The New York Times Company's corporate planning group.

Ali honed her approach to customer experience at her company, Fab Foundations, where she wrote two bestselling books, *Busted* and *Fit My Bras* and created the world's leading bra fitting training and certification program.

Now, Ali lives in Indianapolis with her husband and one very spoiled dog and teaches Entrepreneurship at Purdue University. She also works with clients worldwide to incorporate her innovative customer experience strategies with business advisory, training and speaking through her company Your Iconic Brand, www.youriconicbrand.com

BIBLIOGRAPHY

Part I:

A 2017 study examined customer behavior at consumer-packaged goods companies. This study found that the top 20 percent of customers generated 73 percent of a consumer-packaged goods company's revenue.

Kim, B. J., V. Singh, and R. S. Winer. "The Pareto Rule for Frequently Purchased Packaged Goods: An Empirical Generalization." Marketing Letters, Springer 24(4) (December 2017): 491-507.

In another study, Dan McCarthy, a professor at Emory University, and New York University's Russell Winer also investigated the contribution of companies' most valuable customers.

McCarthy, Daniel and Russell S. Winer. "The Pareto Rule in Marketing Revisited." SSRN (October 10, 2018), https://papers.ssrn.com/sol3/papers.cfm?abstract_id=3264425.

The Harvard Business Review found that it costs five to twenty-five times more for companies to acquire a new customer versus retaining an existing one.

Gallo, A. "The Value of Keeping the Right Customers." Harvard Business Review (2014, November 05), https://hbr.org/2014/10/the-value-of-keeping-the-right-customers.

In fact, the power of customer retention is underscored even further by research from Bain & Co. that shows when companies improve the rate of customer retention by as little as 5 percent, they see an increase in profit that ranges anywhere from 25 percent to 95 percent.

Reichheld, Fred. Prescription for Cutting Costs: Loyal Relationships. PDF. Boston: Bain & Co., September, 2001.

Research shows that people trust positive feedback from people they know.

Perkins, Ben, and Celine Frenech. Consumer Review: The Growing Power of Consumers. PDF. London: Deloitte, 2014.

And people even trust strangers more than reviews from experts.

"Local Consumer Review Survey | Online Reviews Statistics & Trends." BrightLocal (December 7, 2018), https://www.brightlocal.com/research/local-consumer-review-survey/?SSAID=314743&SSCID=31k3_ecpp2#local-business-review-habits.

Back in the 1980s, studies of negative word-of-mouth showed dissatisfied customers telling anywhere from nine to fifteen people about their bad experience, sometimes as many as twenty.

TARP, Consumer Complaint Handling in America: An Update Study, Parts I, II, and III. Washington DC: US Office of Consumer Affairs, 1986.

When an average Facebook user has 338 friends and a viral complaint can reach millions, you ignore the impact of word-of-mouth at your peril.

Smith, Aaron. "What People Like and Dislike about Facebook." Pew Research Center (February 07, 2014), http://www.pewresearch.org/fact-tank/2014/02/03/what-people-like-dislike-about-facebook/.

By 2025, 75 percent of the workforce will be comprised of the newer generations of workers: Millennials and Gen Z.

Dews, Fred. "Brookings Data Now: 75 Percent of 2025 Workforce Will Be Millennials." Brookings. November 29, 2016, https://www.brookings.edu/blog/brookings-now/2014/07/17/brookings-data-now-75-percent-of-2025-workforce-will-be-millennials/.

One Zappos employee even got on a plane to personally deliver fine jewelry that belonged to a customer and was accidentally shipped to the company along with returned merchandise.

Solomon, Micah. "Three Wow Customer Service Stories from Zappos, Southwest Airlines and Nordstrom." Forbes (August 03, 2017), https://www.forbes.com/sites/micahsolomon/2017/08/01/three-wow-customer-service-stories-from-zappos-southwest-airlines-and-nordstrom/#1fa8e6722aba.

Part II:

Research by Zodiac Metrics revealed that "for pretty much every company that we have seen, even those having what are considered 'incredibly loyal' customers, 50-80% of customers transact once and never come back."

Mariychin, Artem. "Five Things You Need to Know About Your Customers to Make Your Startup a Success." Medium (November

27, 2017), https://medium.com/zodiac-metrics/five-things-you-need-to-know-about-your-customers-to-make-your-startup-a-success-2d5384ec79f.

Research by McKinsey & Co has shown that 70 percent of a buying decision is based on how people feel in their interaction with you.

Beaujean, Marc, Jonathan Davidson, and Stacey Madge. "The 'Moment of Truth' in Customer Service." McKinsey & Company (February 2006), https://www.mckinsey.com/business-functions/organization/our-insights/the-moment-of-truth-in-customer-service.

The Journal of Marketing Research also found that brands inspiring higher levels of emotional intensity receive three times more word-of-mouth compared to less emotionally-connected brands.

Taber, Kelsey. "20 Impactful Statistics About Using Testimonials In Marketing." Boast (March 2, 2016), https://boast.io/20-statistics-about-using-testimonials-in-marketing/.

Walker, a customer experience consulting firm, estimates that customer experience will overtake price and product as the key differentiator for brands by 2020.

Gibbons, Patrick, Jeff Marr, Sonya McAllister, Leslie Pagel, and Troy Powell. Customers 2020 The Future of B-to-B Customer Experience. PDF. Indianapolis: Walker, 2013.

According to a recent Gartner Customer Experience in Marketing Survey, more than two-thirds of marketers say their company competes mostly on the basis of customer experience, and 81 percent say they expect to be competing mostly or completely on the basis of customer experience within the next two years.

Ray, Augie, Jane-Anne Mennella, and Simon Yates. "Customer Experience in Marketing Survey 2017: Greater Expectations, Greater Challenges." Gartner (October 05, 2017), https://www.gartner.com/doc/3812767/customer-experience-marketing-survey-.

In the restaurant business, an average restaurant sells somewhere between $300 and $600 per square foot. Cheesecake Factory, which is legendary for its profitability in the restaurant world, sells at around $1,000 per square foot. In comparison, ClusterTruck sells at about $1,600 per square foot.

McGinsie, Cavan. "ClusterTruck: Indy's Food Delivery Revolution." NUVO (May 18, 2016), https://www.nuvo.net/food/clustertruck-indy-s-food-delivery-revolution/article_bcbbaafb-e04c-56c4-9cd5-902a8dd4f39a.html.

"We're seeing that CLV can be a game-changer. Its use cases are growing, and it has the ability to bridge silos, offering a 'gold standard metric' that everyone from marketers, R&D people, HR, and senior executives can share."

"CLV: The Numbers You Need to Know." Executive Education. (October 2015), https://executiveeducation.wharton.upenn.edu/thought-leadership/wharton-at-work/2015/10/clv-numbers-you-need-to-know/.

According to the Nielsen Company's Global Trust in Advertising Survey, "The most credible advertising comes straight from the people we know and trust. More than eight-in-10 global respondents (83%) say they completely or somewhat trust the recommendations of friends and family."

Global Trust in Advertising Winning Strategies for an Evolving Media Landscape. PDF. New York: Nielsen Global Survey, September 2015.

The lifetime value for new referral customers is 16 percent higher than that of customers who came onboard without a referral.

Schmitt, Philipp, Bernd Skiera, and Christophe Van den Bulte. "Referral Programs and Customer Value." Journal of Marketing Research 75 (January 2011), 46 – 59.

84 percent of B2B decision makers start their buying process with a referral.

Minsky, Laurence, and Keith A. Quesenberry. "How B2B Sales Can Benefit from Social Selling." Harvard Business Review (November 8, 2016), https://hbr.org/2016/11/84-of-b2b-sales-start-with-a-referral-not-a-salesperson.

The American Marketing Association estimates that people are exposed to as many as ten thousand brand messages a day

Saxon, J. "Why Your Customers' Attention Is the Scarcest Resource in 2017." American Marketing Association (2017), https://www.ama.org/partners/content/Pages/why-customers-attention-scarcest-resources-2017.aspx.

Part III:

When customers complain to companies, 37 percent are generally satisfied with the interaction when they are offered something of monetary value, such as a refund or credit. But when the business adds an apology to the compensation, satisfaction doubles to 74 percent.

Murcott, Mary. The Customer Rage Study: An Independent Study of Customer Complaint-Handling Experiences. PDF. Highland Park, MI: Dialog Direct, 2015.

Brené Brown is a researcher whose work focuses on vulnerability and shame, which are big inhibitors to growth and leadership. She talks about building trust as being like a marble jar.

Brown, C. Brené. Daring Greatly: How the Courage to Be Vulnerable Transforms the Way We Live, Love, Parent, and Lead. New York, N.Y.: Gotham, 2012.

Part IV:

There are numerous advantages to having engaged employees. In addition to greater job satisfaction, engaged employees have lower absenteeism, higher levels of retention, and they are more likely to be loyal employees. Plus, engaged employees are 17 percent more productive than their less engaged peers.

Hackbarth, Natalie. "14 Benefits of Employee Engagement—Backed By Research." Employee Engagement Software (April 26, 2018), https://www.quantumworkplace.com/future-of-work/14-benefits-of-employee-engagement-backed-by-research.

Inc. magazine talked to executives at six hundred companies, asking them to estimate what percentage of their team would be able to name the company's top three priorities. Executives predicted that 64 percent would successfully be able to name them.

Coyle, Daniel. The Culture Code: The Secrets of Highly Successful Groups. New York, NY: Bantam Books, 2018.

Research from the Local Search Association reveals that the majority of customers expect a company to respond within twenty-four hours.

Sterling, Greg. "Study: Consumers Expect a Review Response within 24 Hours." LSA Insider (September 21, 2018), https://www.lsainsider.com/study-consumers-expect-review-response-within-24-hours/archives.

The effort to respond to customers in a timely manner has a material positive impact on a company's online reputation. According to Harvard Business Review, responding to customer reviews actually improves online ratings.

Proserpio, Davide, and Giorgos Zervas. "Study: Replying to Customer Reviews Results in Better Ratings." Harvard Business Review (February 14, 2018), https://hbr.org/2018/02/study-replying-to-customer-reviews-results-in-better-ratings.

Here's a list of additional books that influenced the writing of Keep Your Customers:

- *Customer Centricity: Focus on the Right Customers for Strategic Advantage* by Peter Fader (Wharton Executive Essentials; May 15, 2012)
- *Delivering Happiness: A Path to Profits, Passion, and Purpose* by Tony Hsieh (Grand Central Publishing; June 7, 2010)
- *O Great One!: A Little Story about the Awesome Power of Recognition* by David Novak and Christa Bourg (Portfolio; May 10, 2016)
- The collective works of Brené Brown

- *The Culture Code: The Secrets of Highly Successful Groups* by Daniel Coyle (Bantam; January 30, 2018)
- *The Happiness Advantage: How a Positive Brain Fuels Success in Work and Life* by Shawn Achor (Currency; September 14, 2010)
- *The Power of Habit: Why We Do What We Do in Life and Business* by Charles Duhigg (Random House; February 28, 2012)
- *Zombie Loyalists Using Great Service to Create Rabid Fans* by Peter Shankman (St. Martin's Press; January 27, 2015)

Printed in the USA
CPSIA information can be obtained
at www.ICGtesting.com
JSHW022330140824
68134JS00019B/1407